MW00510361

From Tee
To Green
To Hollywood

Golfing with the Stars

by Jim Chenoweth
with Bill Kushner

Foreword by Jerry Lewis

Quality Sports Publications

ISBN 1-885758-13-8

Cover designed by Mick McCay
Cover and instructional photos by Dondero Photographic Services
All other photographs compliments of Jim Chenoweth, Jerry Lewis Films and
International Creative Management

For information write or FAX:
Quality Sports Publications
24 Buysse Drive, Coal Valley, IL 61240
(800) 464-1116 • (309) 234-5016 • (309) 234-5019 FAX

Duane Brown, Project Director
Melinda Brown, Designer
Susan Smith, Editor

Printed in the U.S.A.

Publisher's Cataloging-in-Publication Data
Chenoweth, Jim
    From tee to green to Hollywood : golfing with the stars
/ by Jim Chenoweth with Bill Kushner ; foreword by Jerry
Lewis. -- 1st ed.
    p. cm.
    Includes index
    ISBN: 1-885758-13-8
    1. Chenoweth, Jim--Relations with celebrities.
2. Golfers--California--Los Angeles--Biography. 3. Golf--
Unites States--Anecdotes. 4. Golf--United States.
I. Kushner, Bill. II. Title.

GV961.C54A3 1998   796.352'092 [B]
                                   QBI98-882

Dedicated to golf enthusiasts throughout the world.
And to my family and friends, especially
Diane Heltzel, who was the inspiration behind the title
From Tee To Green To Hollywood.

TABLE OF CONTENTS

Acknowledgements

First and foremost, I would like to thank Melinda, Duane and Bill of Quality Sports Publications for taking my scribbled and wrinkled notes and assembling them onto what are now clean pages of text. Without their efforts, my stories would have forever remained scribbled, wrinkled notes. I am grateful.

Secondly, I would like to thank my friends Debbie, Jim, Willie and Sharon of Taylor Made Golf for providing me with the type of incredible technology that keeps me young... at least on the golf course, where my tee shots split fairways and on occasion I even find myself putting for an eagle on a par five. Thank you Taylor Made for the service and equipment that make the game what it should be – a tremendous rush at any age.

And then I would like to say thanks to John and Benny at Red Hawk Golf Club for my home away from home. The best golf equipment in the world isn't worth a hill of beans unless a person has a great golf course to provide the test. I have the best of both worlds.

Next, I started writing a thank you to my many wonderful friends in Hollywood for the good times and memories. But before long I had enough pages for another book. Then I thought, they know. My friends still playing the courses of our world, my friends playing the great golf course of the next... they all know how much I care. They know how much I love them all, especially Jerry Lewis, Bing Crosby and George Burns.

To my family, to my friends, to golfers throughout the world because we are friends... thanks for the memories and thanks for the adventures yet to be.

Foreword

Jim Chenoweth, the teacher of the stars, has been my friend and my pro for quite some time and his teaching methods are by far the most simple while most complete I think you'll find anywhere in the world of golf.

Watching Jim's clinics and teaching techniques while doing exhibitions around the country brought my handicap from a 14 to a 5 in less than a year. Jim has an uncanny ability to learn about you and your needs immediately... Hence he knows how to get the very best out of you while keeping you playing within your capacity.

Jim Chenoweth is not only a great teacher, but one hell of a man... And now he is bringing his many talents and Hollywood experiences to the literary world under the title *From Tee To Green To Hollywood*. I've always believed that sooner or later Jim would do a book about his entertaining, heart warming and hilarious adventures with Hollywood legends. There is no doubt in my mind, this one has got to be well worth the read.

Jerry Lewis

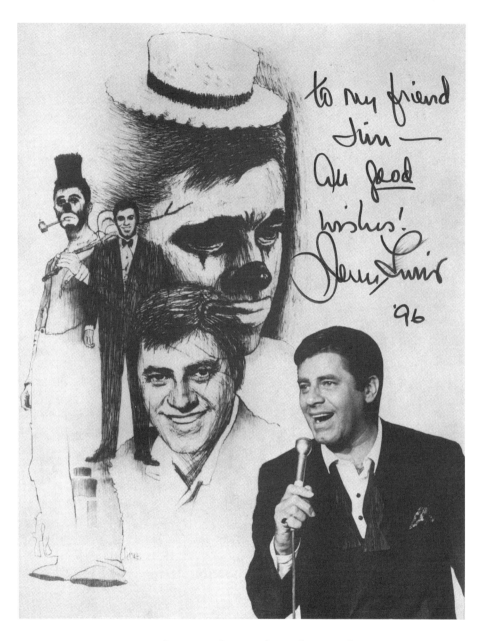

**America's Ambassador of comedy
and my friend, Jerry Lewis.**

Me and Jerry Lewis, Phoenix, Arizona, 1982.

1

Who's Calling
Me At 3:00 A.M?

It came as a gradual interruption from the distance, a somewhat muted clanging of a slow pounding, heavy metal bell. A moment later the sound increased to a God-awful noise. It had become an accelerated ringing in my ears, an echoed noise which shook every fiber of my body, mind and soul.

"Ringing?" I asked the question almost as though I were coming out of a coma. "Yes, ringing... something is ringing." I mumbled to myself while groping about in the darkness.

I wasn't quite sure where I was or, for that matter, who I was. Several moments later things began falling in place. I was being rousted from a deep, deep sleep by this ringing sound.

"The telephone... it's the phone," I said while finally identifying the ringing. "Answer the phone, dummy."

At the very moment I was telling some dummy to answer the phone, I suddenly remembered, I was alone.

I rolled over and looked at the blurred red numbers of the digital clock. I saw a three followed by two zeros.

"Who's calling me at three in the morning?" I asked with a dry, pasty mouth.

Still somewhat groggy, I fumbled with the phone, picked it up and said, "Hello."

"Jim," there was a very alert and excited voice at the other end, a man's voice. "Jim," the voice repeated. "Wake up! This is very important! Sit up and pay attention!"

I wasn't sure this was really happening or if I was simply having a dream. Nonetheless, I sat up in bed and attempted to gather in my senses. This phone call had the ring of something more than simply important. It sounded urgent. Maybe it was some kind of an emergency.

"Are you sitting up?" The man at the other end of the telephone asked.

"Yes," I answered while trying to recognize the voice. I had heard the voice before, but couldn't quite place it.

"Are you wide awake?"

"Well... well... I'm awake," I replied with a little uncertainty.

"Okay, then listen now because this is, and I repeat, very important."

The voice paused and left me hanging. I waited for a moment and then heard the question, "Jim, are you sure you're awake?"

"Yes, I'm awake," I replied. I was getting a little agitated, irked. "I'm awake! Wide awake! Go ahead! Whatever it is, I want to hear it!"

"Jim, don't get mad. I just wanted to be sure you were awake because this is important."

"Well," I settled down a little and continued with my dialogue. "I'm awake. So go ahead." I was now speaking in a softer, rather passive tone. I wanted to hear what was so important.

"I'm sorry, Jim, I had to be sure you were wide awake. It's important you know. Okay, here goes." There was a pause and then, finally, the voice asked, "Why don't blind men sky dive?"

"What?" I asked the question in a rather dumbfounded way.

The voice had the sound of urgency, but the question about blind men sky diving was the first indication something was out of sync. And now, once again I found myself trying to identify the voice. But before my suspicions could gain any momentum, the question came again.

"Why don't blind men sky dive?"

Damn... I had heard the voice before but just couldn't place it. And now, for whatever the reason, perhaps just the urgency of the voice, I found myself drawn into this nighttime madness.

"Why don't blind men sky dive?" I repeated the original question. "I don't know. Why don't blind men sky dive?"

"Sky diving scares the hell out of their dogs," came the answer followed by a dial tone.

It was now 3:02 A.M. I was wide awake, sitting in the middle of my bed and listening to the dial tone. Then it hit me... the voice... why that &%$*#. It was Jerry Lewis.

Well, I wasn't going to let Jerry get away with this one. I turned on the light, grabbed my robe, walked down the hall and into my office, found Jerry's telephone number and dialed with a vengeance.

The line was busy! Fifteen minutes later, I was still getting a busy signal. Finally I gave up and went back to bed.

Twenty minutes ago I was sleeping in the most comfortable bed in the history of beds. Furthermore, I was in a deep sleep, sleeping like a baby. But now I couldn't get comfortable and I couldn't get back to sleep. All I could do was toss and turn and toss and turn. And then, every fifteen minutes or so, I'd glance at the clock.

Did you ever notice that time has a way of passing really slowly when you can't get to sleep?

I punched the pillow a couple of times trying to fluff it up into a comfortable position. Then I thought about punching Jerry a couple of times. Damn... I would get even with him. Someday, I promised myself. I would get even with him.

I tossed and turned for a while longer and then looked at the clock. It was now four fifteen and I was wide awake. I know, I told myself, I'll call Jerry. By now he had probably hung up the phone and went to bed. This would be my opportunity to get even.

Turning on the light, I put on my robe, and walked down the hall with a little more purpose this time. This would be my moment of revenge. Why I could picture Jerry sleeping soundly. And then, I could see him getting pounded by the sound of the bell. "Call me at three in the morning... I'd fix him."

I practiced my speech. My phone call to Jerry would contain no questions about dogs or blind men sky diving. It would be an assault of cuss words and then I'd slam the phone down and let him hear the dial tone.

I dialed, but the line was still busy. I hung up and dialed again just to be sure I hadn't reached a wrong number. It was still busy. Unbelievable! Evidently, Jerry went to bed and never hung up the phone. My revenge would have to wait. But in all of this, there was some good news. I was getting tired.

Making the trip back up the hall, I took off my robe and fell softly into bed. This time everything was comfortable again – the pillow, covers, and bed. I sighed, relaxed and soon started drifting off to sleep.

Suddenly, I heard that noise again. This time I recognized the sound a little quicker. It was the phone again.

I glanced at the clock. It was nearly five in the morning. It couldn't be Jerry I told myself. Even Jerry has to sleep sometime.

Well... I don't know why, but I answered. "Hello."

"Jim, what the hell are you doing up at five o'clock in the morning? A person your age needs his rest. Now go on, get to bed."

It was Jerry and once again I was holding the phone while listening to a dial tone. He got me... again!

That was the first of many early morning phone calls I would receive from Jerry. Sometimes he'd be halfway around the world and call to let me know mother earth was really round. "Jim," he'd say, "I'm standing in the sunshine of high noon. If it's dark where you are, and I suspect it is, then the world really is round."

Naturally he would hang up on me and naturally I'd put on the light, grab my robe, walk down the hall way to my office, find his telephone number and try to call him. I never did get through to Jerry after any of his infamous nighttime calls. And, what's more, unfortunately, I never did get even with Jerry. He had a knack of nailing me when I would least expect and then I would usually forget about revenge.

Oh, there were a few occasions when I would be out at a party and come home rather late... one o'clock, two o'clock in the morning, sometimes even later. I'd pick up the phone and call Jerry. But after one ring, Jerry would answer in a very clear and alert voice. It never seemed to matter what time I called, because it would be obvious to me that Jerry wasn't sleeping. He was always up and wide awake.

To this day, I'm not sure if Jerry ever goes to sleep. I've spent a lot of time with Jerry, and no matter how hard I'd try to stay awake, I'd always conk out before him. But in the morning, Jerry would always be up and ready to go before me. To tell you the truth, I'm not sure if Jerry even owns a bed.

I know many people are amazed during Jerry's Muscular Dystrophy Telethons. He stays up for more than twenty-four hours and never misses a beat. But that's just a normal day in the life of Jerry.

Jerry Lewis, what can I say? Jerry's an amazing guy and has given me a lifetime of memories. In spite of his late night or early morning phone calls, I really love the guy.

Life is not only an interesting journey but a fascinating one, too. There are many times when I sit back and think that had I made a left turn instead of a right one, I probably would have never met Jerry Lewis or some of the other interesting people I've come to know.

What I mean to say is that during the course of life we all have dreams, aspirations and the greatest of plans for tomorrow. But all it takes is one little twist in the road and suddenly we find ourselves catapulted into a different adventure.

Originally, I started out with the dream of playing professional baseball. I kind of liked the idea of hitting that little white ball with a baseball bat.

Then one day I saw a dopey-looking guy hitting a golf ball at the local driving range. I figured if that guy could hit a golf ball then anyone could hit a golf ball. Seriously, how hard could it be?

For openers, a golf ball wasn't curving and twisting through the air at ninety miles an hour. A golf ball was sitting up just asking to be hit. Now how hard could it be to hit a golf ball?

And so, with that simple little question asked but never answered, I put away my baseball bat and glove. I opted for a career change. I'd take the easy way out. After all, it was the logical choice to make. Since I really liked the idea of hitting white balls, I told myself I'd become a professional golfer and hit a ball that wasn't moving.

As a minor league baseball player I was making less than minimum wage. But with the career change at hand, I started to dream about fame and fortune. And why not? I've heard stories that PGA touring pros made nothing but money. I also heard that everyone was after them for endorsements, and endorsements meant even more money. So, that was it. I'd become a touring pro. Seriously, how hard could it be to hit a golf ball?

Since I was a pretty fair athlete, I figured it would take me a day or so to learn all about hitting the golf ball, and then a couple of hours to study up on the rules. After that, I'd turn pro and spend the rest of my life hitting that little white ball and raking in the green.

Okay, I admit, the first time I teed up a ball and swung a club, I missed by a foot or so. But, I was an athlete, a man of talent. And so, how hard could it be to hit a golf ball?

It was a number of years later that I found myself asking the same question while flying from Reno to Phoenix. "Seriously," I mumbled to myself while looking at an empty glass that once contained a martini, "how hard can it be to hit a golf ball?"

"For some people it's really hard," the voice answered my question.

I looked up to see the flight attendant standing next to me. I must have had a bewildered expression on my face because she continued. "You asked, 'how hard can it be to hit a golf ball?' And I answered, 'for some people it's really hard.' Hitting a golf ball takes a lot of coordination and something called talent. If you're thinking of taking up the game of golf, my advice to you is..."

She paused and sort of looked me up and down for a second or two and then continued with her sentence, "don't. It's like I said, hitting a golf ball takes a lot of coordination and talent."

The flight attendant walked away and left me muddling in a little bit of confusion. I think she might have been inferring that I didn't have coordination and talent.

Well, for her information I did have coordination and talent. And furthermore, I was a golfer... a professional golfer. In fact, I was on my way to Phoenix for a big tournament.

"Miss," I got the flight attendant's attention. "Could I see you for a second?"

As she walked over to me, I said, "Perhaps you didn't know, but I am a professional golfer."

"Oh," she said, "forgive me for not recognizing you Mr. Palmer."

I smiled and laughed a little and then said, "I'm not Arnold Palmer. I'm Jim Chenoweth from Reno."

"Jim Chenoweth, from Reno," her voice sounded a little excited. Evidently, she had heard of me. "Sorry, Jim Chenoweth from Reno, but I never heard of you."

"Well," I started to explain, "I won the Nevada Open at Ely, Nevada, three years in a row."

"Wow," she retorted in a acrimonious way, "the Nevada Open at Ely, Nevada. I'm really impressed."

"And I won the Sun Valley Idaho Open two years in a row."

Head professional, Bill Butterfield and me, Jim Chenoweth, the winner of the Sun Valley Open.

"Idaho? Isn't that a potato?"

Oh, she was a funny girl all right, really funny. She really had a sense of humor – a warped sense of humor. But I wasn't deterred.

"And," I continued spouting off my resume, "several years ago, at Twin Falls, I fired a first day 62... it's still the course record."

"And what did you shoot the second day, eighty?" She asked the question with an all-knowing look on her face.

With everyone on the plane staring at me, I wasn't going to answer that question. I think the flight attendant was trying to embarrass me. If I told her the truth, she would have twisted it and everyone on the plane would have been falling into the aisles laughing. Opening with a 62, I was actually lapping the field. But golf is a learning experience and that night, Tony Lema taught me a lesson I never forgot.

Tony was also playing in the tournament. He was earning his stripes, coming up through the ranks, getting ready for the big tour. But after my blazing 62, Tony was a long way back in second place. I had such a commanding lead that it would take a miracle on Tony's part to win the tournament, plus a major collapse on my behalf. Believe me, this one was over and I knew exactly where the trophy was going. And most important, I had already made room in my wallet for the winner's share of the purse.

But after a day on the course, Tony took me out for a "few" drinks. A few drinks became many drinks and many drinks became an all-night affair. Whereas Tony nursed a couple of drinks for the entire night, I took the plunge. Hey, I was celebrating my 62. I was celebrating my victory. I had won the tournament on the first day.

In the morning, I staggered to the first tee, teed up a single golf ball but saw three. Attempting to hit the ball closest to me, I toed one out of bounds. And that opening drive turned out to be one of my better shots during the next several holes.

Finally, on the third or maybe the fourth hole my caddie figured everything out. Realizing I was hung-over he said, "If you're seeing three balls aim for the one in the middle."

It helped a little, but I went on to shoot a second day 82.

I stayed away from the bars for the next two nights and finished with a 67 and a 68. Tony Lema won the tournament and went on to the PGA Tour. As for myself, here I was, avoiding the answer to the last question the flight attendant had just asked.

"You did hack up the course the second day, didn't you?" She asked the question almost as though she knew the answer. Suddenly her voice was bubbling in laughter. "Now I understand. You're not really a professional golfer. You're a club pro." She rolled her eyes back a little and sort of chuckled to herself. "A club pro."

"A club pro, yes, but I still earn my living as a professional golfer."

"Earn your living?" She was laughing so loud that if everyone on the plane wasn't looking at us before, then they were certainly looking at us now. "My ex-boyfriend earned his living as a club pro, too. But neither one of us enjoyed starvation so he quit the club pro business in lieu of a career that paid in money and not free range balls. He went into minor league baseball."

And with that statement, the flight attendant walked away laughing. I could have fired back and told her that I played minor league baseball, too. And I could have told her that I made more money as a club pro than I did in the minor leagues. Being a club pro wasn't just free range balls. I got free golf, too, and no one was throwing fast balls at my face.

Actually, I could have really let her have it... but I was too much of a gentleman to engage in that sort of stuff. Besides, she did have a pretty quick and smart mouth. And it wasn't much fun to have people laughing at you instead of laughing with you.

I glanced at the guy sitting across the aisle from me. He tipped his glass which obviously contained an adult beverage and said, "Cheers."

I tipped my empty glass and replied, "Yeah, dittos."

Damn, I just couldn't believe the shoddy treatment I was receiving from a flight attendant. As my mind was going over recent events, I suddenly thought about the guy across the aisle from me. He was familiar.

I looked at him, but his head was turned. He was looking out the window. Then I noticed there were several empty glasses on his tray and I only had one. What gives here?

"Miss." I got the flight attendant's attention once again.

She glared at me from several seats away and asked, "Now what do you want, Mr. Snead?"

Lifting my empty martini glass I said, "My glass is empty..."

"So, what do you expect me to do?"

"I'd like another martini, please."

Walking back toward my seat, she explained, "Look, Mr. Hogan, it's one drink per customer per flight."

"But that man sitting over there," I whispered and pointed toward the gentleman across the aisle from me, "has more than one empty glass on his tray."

"Well that man sitting across the aisle from you isn't a club pro. He's a celebrity. A star. A rich and famous person. He's married to Betty Grable. That's Harry James."

"Harry James," I said with a bit of awe in my voice as I leaned forward trying to take a peek at him. "Harry James, the greatest trumpet player in the world."

Harry was still looking out the window as the flight attendant turned to him and asked, "Mr. James, would you like another drink?"

"Why yes, thank you," Harry said in a casual manner.

The flight attendant ran up the aisle to get Harry another drink as he leaned over toward me and said, "The service on this flight is fantastic.

And she's an absolute gemstone. Isn't she?"

Before I could answer the question, the flight attendant had returned with Harry's drink. He glanced over at me, tipped his glass and said, "Cheers."

"Yeah," I said once again as I tipped my empty glass, "Dittos."

"Here, here," Harry sat up. "Your glass is empty. Miss," he looked at the flight attendant, "bring my friend a drink. You're drinking martinis, right?"

"Well, yeah, I'm drinking martini, as in singular. Didn't you know it's one drink per customer per flight?" I looked at the flight attendant.

"That's nonsense," Harry laughed. "Let's make sure we get you into the plural. Miss, bring my friend a couple of martinis."

While the flight attendant went for my drinks, Harry stuck out his hand and said, "I'm Harry James. And aren't you Jim Chenoweth, professional golfer from Reno?"

I was surprised! Shocked! Imagine that, Harry James recognized me.

Sitting up straighter, and with a little pride in my voice, I replied, "Yep, I'm Jim Chenoweth, professional golfer from Reno."

Obviously, Harry had heard about me. Or maybe Harry had seen me play in a tournament. Or maybe Harry was there when I won a tournament.

Just as I was ready to ask Harry how he knew me, he said, "I thought that's what I heard you tell the flight attendant when she was going off on you. And, about our flight attendant... well, I've been on her flights before and she's always picking on someone. It's just her personality."

Harry explained that our flight attendant actually picked on him the first couple of times he was on her flight. Then one day, he was traveling with his wife, Betty Grable.

"When she recognized Betty," Harry was saying, "I suddenly became her favorite trumpet player. Win the Masters, Jim, and you'll be her favorite golfer."

With drinks in hand, Harry and I began to talk. It turned out he was on his way to Phoenix for the same tournament, the Scottsdale Pro-Am. Actually, it was a big tournament which featured touring pros, movie stars and Jim Chenoweth, professional golfer from Reno.

Once we landed Harry suggested, "Jim, since we're both going to the Scottsdale Country Club, why not cancel your limo and ride over in mine."

Canceling my limo meant I wouldn't be riding to Scottsdale in a bus or taxi cab. I told Harry to consider my limo canceled and with that we started looking for his ride.

Before long, Harry had everyone looking for his limo without any results. After about fifteen minutes and no limo, Harry started mumbling about incompetency. He said that someone was always screwing up his limo rides from airports to hotels.

After about thirty minutes it became evident that no limo would be coming. I flagged a cab and Harry and I were off to Scottsdale.

At the Scottsdale Country Club, Harry ran into another problem with incompetency. Harry's reservation was screwed up. He didn't have a room, and the place was booked solid.

"It's another case of incompetency, Jim. Incompetency," Harry said. "I can't get limos to pick me up at airports and hotels are always screwing up my reservations."

Actually, Harry was calm about everything and the man working the front desk said that he would see what he could do. In the meantime, Harry needed something to drink and headed for the bar.

Just as soon as Harry was out of sight the clerk said, "That's his problem, you know."

I didn't understand what the clerk meant.

"The sauce," he said. "Mr. James had the same problem last year when he came in for the tournament. We figured that he gets to drinking and forgets about little things such as making reservations and calling us with his schedule so that we can send a limo to the airport."

The clerk continued. He told me that Harry never responds to the invitation to play in the tournament, but usually shows up when everyone is ready to tee off. "He's actually early this year. But, I don't know what we're going to do because there are no rooms."

Since I won the tournament a few years ago, I was sort of a hero at the Scottsdale Country Club. That meant whenever I was in town they would give me a luxury suite. Hey, I just thought of something. Where was that flight attendant now?

With plenty of room in my suite, I went into the bar, found Harry stacking up martini glasses, and told him my idea. "It's a big suite, Harry... plenty of room... So, why not stay with me?"

Once we were unpacked, Harry found the liquor cabinet and made a couple of drinks for us. As I passed on the drink I told Harry my 62-82 story. Then I said, "I hope you don't mind drinking alone, but whenever I'm playing in a tournament, I don't touch the stuff after sundown."

Harry shrugged his shoulders and said, "Sundown, sun up or high noon, I not only touch the stuff but I drink it, too."

After slamming down both drinks, Harry unpacked his trumpet. "And now, Jim, I hope you don't mind, but I have to keep my lip sharp."

Harry then proceeded to take out his teeth and blast a few notes on the trumpet. Suddenly he stopped playing, looked at me and smiled.

"I exercise my lip this way every night. I take out the ol' trumpet and play a few notes. It makes for a stronger lip."

That night I went to sleep as the greatest trumpet player in the world piped soft brass notes.

The next morning, I heard the knock on the door. It was room service.

Harry was already up and had ordered breakfast for both of us.

During breakfast, Harry would take a bite of food and down it with a drink. My god, it was a little bite of food and a big drink. And I'm not talking orange juice, either.

While watching Harry drink breakfast, I could only wonder what pro would end up with him as a partner? You see, the tournament was called the Scottsdale Pro-Am. That meant that as an amateur, Harry would be paired with a professional golfer.

As he continued to slam down one drink after the other, I wanted to cry for the pro Harry would be partnered with. After all, I wasn't quite sure that Harry would be able to stand upright after breakfast much less even see a golf ball. What a thought – playing in a tournament with Harry as a partner.

Don't get me wrong, because Harry was a terrific guy. But with the amount of alcohol he had just consumed, I had nothing but pity for the poor sap who drew Harry as a partner.

"Oh, by the way, Jimmy boy," Harry said as he slammed another drink down, "I checked with the tournament director about the pairings. And guess who I drew as a partner?"

One of the classiest guys I have ever met, Harry James.

2

If Harry Was A Trumpeter, Then Betty Was A Pitcher

From my own personal, one-time experience, I knew that drinking and driving didn't mix. I'm not talking about drinking and driving the freeways either. I'm talking about drinking and attempting to drive a golf ball off the first tee... or any tee for that matter.

It was a natural reaction, but at breakfast, when Harry James confirmed that he and I had been partnered at the Scottsdale Pro-Am, my only hope was that he wouldn't stagger and fall down on the way to the practice range. I didn't want to see Harry hurt himself or worse yet, injure someone in the crowd with an errant shot.

Well, we left the room and Harry never staggered. Instead, he walked with the brisk swagger of a confident general en route to battle. He never missed a step as he said, "I'm really looking forward to getting out on the course and hitting a few with you, Jimmy Boy."

Of course, there was no doubt in my mind that once we got to the driving range and Harry bent over to tee up a ball, his world would go into a serious tail spin. I'm talking about blurred vision, you know teeing up one golf ball but seeing three.

Well... I was prepared for everything and anything. When it all hit Harry, and I was positive it would, that's when my voice of experience would step in and tell him to aim for the ball in the middle and not to worry if the world tilted and he fell off. I'd be there to catch him.

Fortunately, today was only the practice round. The tournament, a two-day, thirty-six hole affair, would begin tomorrow. With that in mind, I planned to let Harry hack up the course today. But once the practice round was in the books, I'd tell Harry the story about a golfer shooting a 62, partying all night with Tony Lema, and coming back the next day to fire an 82. I wouldn't mention any names, of course. I'd just let Harry know that it was a true story and I knew the dummy who set that record for inconsistency.

Approaching the driving range, I ran into Cliff Whittle, the head pro at Scottsdale Country Club. "Jim," he said while shaking my hand, "I just called your room. I got something going and we can make a few extra bucks, partner."

Cliff had a little money match going. "It's a lock, Jim," Cliff was saying. "You and me against Dutch Harrison, Johnny Bulla."

Dutch was known as the Arkansas Traveling Man. Dutch would go anywhere for a game of golf. And as for Johnny Bulla... well, Johnny played a lot of golf with a guy named Sam Snead.

Make no mistake about it, Dutch and Johnny were pros and anything could happen. But I had played against them before and just seemed to always have their numbers.

I didn't know if it was a lock, but I felt the worst case scenario would be a "break-even day." However, a best case scenario could mean that someone else had paid my expenses for the tournament. Since this wasn't the PGA Tour, and since I was on a budget, a limited budget, I was just about ready to tell Cliff, let's do it.

Then, I saw Harry out of the corner of my eye. I realized we had a little problem. It had to do with five people playing in the same group. Since five-somes were not permitted, I had to pass on the money match.

Cliff was quick to point out that Harry could find another group for his practice round. But I glanced at Harry and immediately came to the conclusion that leaving him at this particular time wasn't the right thing to do.

First of all, I was convinced that once breakfast hit home, Harry was going to need someone to help him back to the room. And secondly, Harry was beginning to remind me of a sad basset hound. Here he was, a star, a famous person and yet he just stood back and looked at me with those sad eyes. My God, he looked like a lost soul. I just couldn't leave Harry... No, I just couldn't do that.

"Hey, Jimmy," Harry said, "go ahead and play. I'll be okay."

Harry was a perceptive guy and I'm sure he had to know I wanted to play in a little money match. But...

"Don't worry about me," Harry said. "I'll be okay. Seriously, Jimmy, I'll find a game."

"Yeah," Cliff said, "Harry will pick up a game."

No, Harry wouldn't pick up a game. I had a feeling he wasn't the kind of a person who could just bogart into someone elses game. If I played with Cliff and the boys, I was sure Harry would just go back to the room and start lifting martini glasses.

I told Cliff, "Thanks, but Harry and I have to get ready for the Pro-Am."

My God, you should have seen the smile come over Harry's face. He looked like a kid on Christmas morning when Santa left a bag full of toys.

A second later Cliff took off looking for another partner as Harry and I completed our walk to the driving range. But then, Harry made a simple statement, something that went in one ear and out the other. Harry said, "You're a pretty good guy, Jimmy. And I won't forget."

At the time, little did I know that my gesture of fair play would not only cement my relationship with Harry James, but it was about to open a new corridor of life through which I would soon be traveling.

Getting back to business, I thought I would have to point Harry down range. You know, sort of make sure he was aiming in the right direction.

To my astonishment, to my utter disbelief, Harry began hitting balls in the right direction without my help. And what's more, he never toed one, never swung and missed one, or never so much as wobbled. In fact, he even bent over, teed up the ball and hit one dead solid perfect.

Remarkable, I told myself. And remarkable it was, I was there when Harry drank his breakfast. And yet, I was watching a physical impossibility. Harry was unfazed. Instead of blurring his vision, Harry's breakfast seemed to focus him.

If Harry was remarkable on the driving range, then he was amazing on the golf course. Harry claimed to be a 13 handicap, but on that particular day he played to a single digit. It wasn't so long ago that I found myself pitying the poor sap who drew Harry as a partner, and now, lucky me. After watching Harry play the course as though it were his trumpet, I was beginning to think that maybe we could win this tournament.

When Harry's last putt hit the bottom of the cup, his scorecard read 77. I called him "Sandy," as in sandbagger. But Harry smiled and said, "You bring out the best in me, Jimmy. The next time there's a money match around here, let's you and me pluck the pigeons."

That night, back at the room, Harry would play a few notes on the trumpet, take a little drink, and then we'd talk. We talked about everything – golf, business, and people in general. Needless to say, Harry was able to not only hit the high notes on the trumpet, but he carried on an intelligent conversation and never spilled so much as a drop of booze.

Eventually I summoned the courage to mention such things as oil and water and inebriated and golf. "Seriously, Harry, I once knew a dummy who shot an opening day 62, went out and partied all night, and came back to embarrass himself with an 82 the very next day. Drinking and golf is just like oil and water. They don't mix."

Harry looked at me with a wry grin and said, "So that's why you don't drink after sundown during a tournament, eh, Jimmy."

What could I say? Yes, Harry was a perceptive guy.

"Ah, but Jimmy boy, let me explain something to you. There's a big difference between drinking and being drunk," Harry said as he slammed down a martini. "You see, I drink, and I drink a lot, but I've never been drunk."

Right or wrong, Harry went on to explain that many years ago he discovered a little drink relaxed him before he played the trumpet. And he carried the same approach over to his game of golf.

"Relax and have fun, Jimmy. Now granted, perhaps if I wasn't so deeply involved with relaxation and fun, I might be a better golfer. But then again, my future and livelihood will never come down to a three-foot putt on the last hole of the tournament. And you've got to admit, a little relaxation and fun hasn't hampered my lip."

Harry lifted the trumpet to his lips and suddenly the room was shaking with the highest note I had ever heard. Yes, I had to admit it. Harry James was the greatest.

Harry and I won the Scottsdale Pro-Am that year and we won it going away. As the professional of our two man team, my prize came in the form of green stuff with pictures of Lincoln, Grant and good ol' Ben Franklin. And Ben Franklin, just for the record, was my favorite.

After the banquet was over, Harry and I went back to the room. I sat down at the table and started sorting through and counting those pictures of dead presidents and my buddy Ben. But Harry just stood back, and with a drink in his hand, he kept looking at his prize, a trophy. It just didn't seem fair – me with the cash and Harry with the trophy. But that's why they call it a Pro-Am.

Slowly, I scooped up the money and put it away. There was no sense in flaunting my winnings in front of Harry.

But then, Harry looked at me and said, "Jimmy, I know cash is cash, but if you tried to trade me all of that money for this trophy I wouldn't do it."

I didn't say anything but I wouldn't make that kind of trade either.

"This trophy means a lot to me," Harry continued.

"Well, Harry," I said in a joking way, "I have a home full of trophies. If you want to make a trade... you know... cash for trophies, I'll be happy to sit down and discuss it with you."

Harry laughed and then went on to explain what the trophy meant to him. It was something that he won. It was first place! It meant a couple of days of good memories. It would always be there to remind him of these days and new friends.

Harry poured me a drink, lifted his glass and said, "Here's to new friends."

The tournament was over and so we drank to new friends.

"I've had a great time," Harry was saying. "And it's due to the fact that you're a good guy, Jim. You made this whole trip better than I ever expected it would be."

Then Harry looked around the room almost as though he wanted to be sure we were alone. And after that, he started to whisper about doing me a big favor. "I'm going to share something with you, Jimmy, something that can put you on easy street for the rest of your life. But you've got to promise me you won't tell a soul. If this information got out, then it would be worthless. So you've got to promise you won't tell anyone about it."

Of course, I promised Harry I wouldn't tell a soul. Not even my wife. No one! I certainly wasn't going to hurt my chances for a lifetime stay on easy street.

When Harry was positive my lips were sealed, he said, "I'll show you the secret tomorrow. It's sort of a career move for you, Jimmy. A big money career move."

I quizzed Harry for a while, but he said nothing more than, "I'll show you the secret tomorrow."

I called my wife and told her the good news. "Write the checks and pay all the bills. We won the tournament." Then I told her I'd be staying over another day or so. I didn't elaborate. I let her know Harry wanted to discuss a career move that would make life easier for us.

That night curiosity got the best of me and I tried to pry the information out of Harry, but he wouldn't budge. He said he'd show me in the morning and that was it. I did get one thing out of him though. And that was, he had learned this guarded secret from Bing Crosby.

Harry James, Bing Crosby, I thought as I laid in bed and stared up at the ceiling. Both men were successful and wealthy. There had to be something to all of this, something big, something that really would put me on easy street for the rest of my life.

The next morning, instead of telling me the secret, Harry and I headed to the track. I'm talking about the kind of track where they have ponies. Do you know what I mean? The race track.

With Harry being Harry and having connections galore, we were soon roaming around the stables talking to trainers and watching the horses. I still didn't know the guarded secret, but remained confident there was a method to whatever Harry was doing. When the time was right, Harry would point me in the direction of easy street.

After about fifteen minutes, Harry seemed to really perk up. He leaned over to me and whispered, "There it is, Jimmy. There's our ticket to easy street. It's sort of like finding our pot of gold at the end of the rainbow."

In a rather secretive way, Harry nodded toward the far end of the stable. I looked, but it was a stable and nothing else. I didn't see a ticket booth where they sold tickets to easy street. I didn't see a rainbow. And I certainly didn't see a pot of gold. I didn't understand.

"There," Harry whispered. "The horse at the end of the stable."

Still, I didn't understand. There was a horse at the end of the stable. Well, at least I saw the back half of a horse at the end of the stable sticking out of a stall. And this back half of the horse was busy doing what the back half of horses normally do.

Surely, I thought, Harry was looking at something other than the droppings of a horse. But to my amazement, he wasn't. Harry was staring at the end product of a grazing horse. Suddenly, my promised trip to easy street was starting to smell.

Harry grinned and maintained, "There she is, Jimmy, our pot of gold."

Although my eyesight was perfect and I had tremendous vision when it came to recognizing potential, I couldn't see the glitter of gold reflecting from that ever-growing pile on the stable floor. Furthermore, if that was our ticket to easy street, then Harry was going to make that trip by himself.

"I don't know what you think you see, but I'm looking at a pile of..."

Harry quickly interrupted me, "Not the crap on the floor, Jimmy. It's the horse. Look at the horse."

Harry explained that Bing Crosby owned a stable of horses in Rancho Santa Fe, California. And one day, as they were visiting the Del Mar Race Track, Bing told Harry about a theory he had, a theory about horses and the trip to easy street.

"It made sense to me," Harry said. "After all, the horse wouldn't be running with extra weight. And what's more, the horse would be relaxed and ready to go. I'm telling you Jimmy, when I'm relaxed I play my best."

Well, Harry wasn't a race horse running at a track. He was a trumpeter. I failed to see the connection between Harry and a race horse, but, I can't say that I was completely negative on the theory. When I thought about it, the horse would be lighter and perhaps that would make a difference.

"Did you and Bing test the theory?"

"Ah, not really. We sat in the bar at Del Mar and did a lot of talking about it. By the time we did get around to making a bet, the racing was over."

At the time, I didn't know Bing Crosby or anything about his social habits. But I had gotten to know Harry. If Bing Crosby was anything like Harry, then I had to ask the obvious question. "How many drinks did you and Bing have before discussing this theory?"

Harry never answered my question. Instead, he asked one of the hands working at the stable the name of the horse and what race she was running in. When I heard the name of the horse, I nearly fell over.

The stable hand, an old, colored gentleman, looked at the horse and said, "We're gonna get her ready now. She'll be runnin' in the first race. That's Pot of Gold."

"Pot of Gold," Harry repeated the name and looked at me in a sobering way. "Is that telling us something, Jimmy?"

Standing at the window and placing my bet, I was still a little reluctant to follow Harry's advice. He wanted me to bet everything I had on a "theory." Sure, Harry's theory seemed to have a little merit, and the horse was Pot of Gold. But with those 99 to 1 odds staring me in the face, I just wasn't willing to risk all of my golf course winnings on one horse.

I placed a fifty dollar bet on Pot of Gold and told Harry, "Let's test the water a little before we jump all the way in."

"Test nothing," Harry said as he crowded against the window and plopped down a wad that really could choke a horse.

"And they're off!"

Several minutes later, Harry and I were standing in the crowd and straining to see the finish line. All the horses were clustered together from beginning to end. It was an exciting race! A photo finish! And from our vantage point we couldn't tell who won much less see if Pot of Gold was in the mix.

I told myself she had to be somewhere in the middle of it all. My God, if Harry hit on a 99 to 1 long shot hit, and I missed this action, I'd ask him to kick me in the back side.

Then I glanced toward my left and saw a horse trotting on the track, sort of moseying toward the finish line. Oh, she looked relaxed, all right, lighter too... But most trotters seem to have that bounce. There she was, Pot of Gold, out for a Sunday stroll when all the other horses were running a race.

I ripped up my ticket, threw it away and shook my head back and forth in disbelief. But Harry still had his eyes closed, fingers crossed and was waiting to hear them announce the winner. I hated to be the one to tell him Pot of Gold wasn't even in the stretch run yet. Hell, they were getting the horses ready for the second race and Pot of Gold was still out on the track.

"You boys back again," the stable hand said as he saw Harry and I studying the back side of other horses.

"Yeah we're back again," I said with the exuberance in my voice waning.

Harry was still positive he was onto something, but I wasn't. I mean to say when the other horses in the race have rounded the first turn and your horse isn't out of the gate yet, something is seriously wrong. Instead of finding a ticket to easy street, I was beginning to suspect that Harry had entered the fast lane to the poor house.

In the natural event of things, Harry and I watched as another horse produced a pot of gold. Or should I say a pile, a weighty pile? This one was the mother load.

"There, Jimmy, that was the problem with Pot of Gold," Harry advanced his theory in a voice brimming with excitement. "She didn't finish taking care of business before she raced. This time, Jimmy, I got a good feeling. Watch and you'll see. This horse will finish her business and it will be a lock."

When Harry was positive the second horse had finished taking care of business, we were back at the window placing our bets. Yes, we, Harry and me, placed our bets. And this time, Harry's wad was big enough to choke an elephant. But mine was a meager twenty dollar wager which drew a disgusted look from Harry.

"Jimmy," he said, "this is a thirty-to-one lock and you're only betting a twenty."

Harry sounded like he knew what he was talking about. He even looked as though he knew something that I didn't. Maybe he was right. Maybe this horse would win.

I bumped my bet to one hundred dollars and promised myself that if I won, I wouldn't bet another race today. I even let God know that if I won, I'd drop a little something extra in the collection plate next time I was in church.

"And they're off!"

Well, at least most of the horses were off. Our horse, on the other hand, stumbled out of the gate and quickly ended any sense of mystery. Here we were, five seconds into the race, and already I knew, our horse was out of it. Maybe Harry didn't understand just yet, but the only "lock" was our horse finishing last.

Right about now, I was beginning to suspect that there might be a hole in Harry's theory.

As we headed back to the stables, I was mentally kicking myself in the back side. How stupid could I be? Oh, I wasn't stupid because I made that first bet. And I wasn't stupid because I bumped up my second bet. I was stupid because I got out of bed this morning.

"I was kind of expectin' to see you guys again," the stable hand said as Harry plunged into the bowels of the stables looking for his next pot of gold.

As for myself, I took a little pride in the knowledge that I was too smart to follow Harry's lead. I sat down on a bench, stared at the ground and shook my head back and forth. My God, I had a wife and a kid. The money I had blown on Harry's theory could have gone a long way in paying some bills. Or maybe I could have done something nice for the family. Hell, even if my wife and I burned the money in the fireplace on a chilly morning, it would have been better served.

"Havin' a bad day, huh?" the stable hand said as he sat next to me. "At first you boys had me stumped. You know, walkin' around here secret like and then runnin' out to make a bet. But then, as I was shovelin' up the horseshit, I figured it out."

We talked, and of course, the old man knew exactly what Harry and I were doing. "Yeah," he said, "I seen it all before... many times. Damn fools come in here, watch a horse take a dump and then run out and make their bets. Why if I had a nickel for every time I saw some fool doin' what you boys were doin',' I'd be on easy street today."

"Easy street," I repeated his words as my shoulders slumped a little lower. "That's where he said we were going... to easy street. He was so positive his theory would work."

My newly found friend laughed and then asked, "Have you ever got up off a toilet and run away?"

"Well..." I said, as I gave a little thought to the question, "I can't think of any times right off hand."

"That's right and you never will think of any times, either," the old man said. "But," he leaned over and with an expression that must have reflected the wisdom of Solomon, he asked, "How many times have you run like hell to get to the toilet?"

It was a revelation. My goodness, he was right. The secret was finding a horse that would soil the stable floor after the race.

"Yep," he said, "that's the secret... finding a horse that's thinking about the toilet as he comes out of the gate. But, don't tell your friend that or he'll be sleeping in the stables looking for a constipated horse."

We continued our dialogue and I learned the horses were unpredictable. The old stable hand said there was no way to know when a horse was ready to go. "Believe me, I've watched the horses before the race and after the race and there just ain't know way to know."

I sat up a little straighter, looked at the old man, and smiled. "All be darn. Why you must have seen it all."

"Yes sir, I've seen guys like you come in here, wait and watch and then run out and make the bet. Then, they're right back in here waitin' and watchin' and suddenly they know the reason they lost the first race. The pile wasn't big enough."

"Yeah," I said with an agreeing nod. "We were looking for a bigger pile."

"See. It never fails. And I can tell you the reason your buddy will come out of the stable thinking he has the winner for the next race."

I never said a word. I just looked at the old man with my face asking the question.

And with a whimsical expression, he finally said, "Horses do a lot of eatin' and whole lot of drinkin' water. So, if the first pile wasn't big enough and the second pile was, but you still lost the race, then... what else is left for the horse to do?"

Before I could say, *take a leak,* I heard Harry's excited voice echo throughout the stables, "Jimmy, I got it now. We only had it half right."

As Harry was coming out of the stables the old man said, "Neither one of us know the winner of the next race, but I have a feeling your buddy sure got the inside track on the loser. And knowing the loser makes it a tad easier pickin' the winner."

As we flew from Phoenix to Las Vegas, Harry was busy downing his martinis and searching for the missing factor in his equation of easy street. Although he lost every race and lost big, Harry was still absolute in his conviction that he was onto something. I tried to tell him what the stable hand had said. But Harry's response was, "The Wright Brothers failed a few times before they got that plane to fly. No, Jimmy, we're onto something. Believe me, this one will work."

I pretended to nod in agreement and then mumbled to myself, "Yeah, it will work, Harry. But so do four leaf clovers and lucky charms."

Landing in Las Vegas, Harry and I said our good-byes but with the promise we'd get together again and soon. In fact, Harry was going to set up some golf – Harry, me and Bing Crosby. It sounded like a great idea.

Harry said we could fly into San Diego, stay with Bing, play some golf and test *our* theory on the ponies. As I turned and headed to the gate for my second leg of the journey to home, I yelled back to Harry, "*Your* theory, Harry. You can test *your* theory."

Arriving at the gate, I discovered the connecting flight to my home in Elko, Nevada, had been canceled. The next flight out would be tomorrow morning – maybe.

Since Elko wasn't considered a tourist hot-spot, it was hard to get out of town and even more difficult getting home. Just as I was ready to make arrangements for a Reno to Elko flight, I bumped into Harry. It was difficult to believe, but, someone screwed up his limo reservations

"Someone screwed up your limo reservation. Gee, Harry, I wonder how that could have happened?"

"But wait a second," Harry quickly changed the subject. "Since your flight's been canceled, you can spend the night at our place... meet Betty and we'll go out to dinner. And better yet, we can squeeze in a round of golf. I live on the course – the Desert Inn."

Wow! I thought, meet Betty Grable. I was going to meet Betty Grable.

When we arrived at Harry's home, my eagerly anticipated meeting with the queen of motion pictures, Betty Grable, would have to wait. No one was there.

Harry unpacked his trophy and put it on a shelf near the bar in his recreation room. Harry was sure proud of that trophy.

"Betty thinks I'm nuts for playing in these golf tournaments. So I'm going to put this trophy where she can see it," Harry said.

We went into the kitchen and Harry fixed us a quick lunch. It was a sandwich and Coke for me, but Harry said something about his liquid diet. I understood. He wanted to relax a little.

Ten, maybe fifteen minutes later, we stepped out the back door, jumped into Harry's golf cart and drove out onto a fairway. Harry was right, he did live on the Desert Inn course.

The course was empty, so Harry dropped a few balls on the ground and asked me several questions about shot making. Actually, he wanted a lesson. I obliged.

I gave him a few pointers on the shoulder turn and making everything a little more compact during the swing. Harry had a tendency to get wristy and he seemed to flail at the ball instead of striking it.

After about twenty minutes of lessons, we headed for the first tee. Harry was a quick learner, and a terrific student. He was excited about the little change I had made in his swing and wanted to test it. Well... we tested it all right – twenty-seven holes of testing. If the sun hadn't gone down, I think Harry would have tested his newly discovered swing for another eighteen holes.

Since it was too dark to see the balls, we drove back to Harry's place. Now, I was finally on my way to met Betty Grable. I could hardly wait.

I never told Harry but I had been a long time fan of Betty's. During those days, what guy wasn't a Betty Grable fan?

Perhaps I should explain that I was a real fan. Why, I knew her full name, Elizabeth Ruth Grable. I knew she was training at the Hollywood Professional School when she was only twelve. And by the time she was fourteen, she was dancing in the chorus lines of Hollywood musical films. From there, the great Sam Goldwyn signed her and the rest was history.

I followed Harry through the kitchen and into the rec room. And suddenly, there she was, near the bar, looking at Harry's trophy. There was an overhead spotlight beaming down on Betty as she stood silent just looking at Harry's trophy.

I had entered a slow moving world where a second of passing time actually seemed like an eternity. At that instant, the thought hit me. Betty Grable was an inspiration for American soldiers during World War II. Our boys painted pictures of Betty on bombers. They talked about her legs, perfectly shaped legs – legs which were insured for a million dollars. Our ground troops carried her photos into battle. Right about now, I had to be the envy of every guy who ever saw her movies or looked at her pictures and said, "Wow."

Then Betty turned toward Harry and I noticed her movie star complexion wasn't due to make-up and special cameras. Her complexion was actually flawless. She was every bit as beautiful in person as she was in the movies. I was looking at the twentieth centuries version of Helen of Troy. Better yet, Betty Grable was our Cleopatra.

It was astounding, but this was Betty Grable. A movie star! A legend! A princess! A queen! A vision of heavenly beauty!

Suddenly I snapped back to reality as Harry said, "Hi babe, I'm home."

Betty didn't say a word. She just stared at Harry in a peculiar way, a dreamy way. Then she glanced at me and I watched as her lips began to form words. I was about to hear her speak for the first time.

"Okay, I know him," she pointed at Harry while looking directly at me. "But who the &%# are you?"

Betty Grable sure had a strange way of making me, one of Harry's friends, feel at home. Oh, I had felt cold shoulders before, but this welcome was a little cooler than Antarctica in the dead of winter.

Then it hit me. That wasn't a dreamy look in Betty's eyes. No sir, she had been consuming adult beverages. You know, drinking as in drunk.

Harry quickly asserted himself like any man would. "Please, sweetheart, this is Jim Chenoweth. He was my partner in the tournament. We won first place, darling."

I understood Harry's approach to the problem standing in front of him. On occasion I had been there myself. We all have. You know, playing a few extra holes of golf when you should have been home. So, I just stood back and watched as Harry licked Betty's boots.

It seemed as though Harry was scoring points because Betty was looking at me in a more relaxed way. Obviously she was beginning to understand that Harry and I were buddies... that we won the tournament. "So, you're another one of his f&%#, a#@ hole golfin' buddies."

Harry said some things and Betty said some things and I listened. Sure, I had heard truck driver language before. I had even taken a course myself – Truck Driver Language 101. But in this verbal jousting of guttural sounds, Harry was seriously overmatched. It was obvious to me that Harry was a novice and Betty had her PhD.

It didn't take Harry long to run up the white flag. His voice sounded retreat as he apologized and then said, "Okay, dear. Now, fix us a drink while Jim and I get cleaned up. And then we'll all go out to eat. I promised Jimmy we'd take him to dinner."

Harry was still in the middle of saying the word *dinner* when he suddenly shouted, "Duck!"

Fowl, I thought. I hope not, I was in the mood for a big thick steak.

Actually, everything really happened quickly. Harry said "dinnerduck." And Betty said, "Fix your own f&%$# drinks," and threw a bottle of bourbon at us.

Suddenly I realized Harry wasn't talking about a bird when he said, "duck!"

Just as the bottle of bourbon exploded against the wall, Betty fired an ashtray in the direction of Harry's head. When I realized Betty could pitch with either hand, I did exactly what Harry had instructed me to do. I ducked behind the sofa.

The air space in Harry's rec room was crowded. Betty was throwing bottles, ashtrays and glasses. Betty could really pitch, but Harry, on the other hand, wasn't much of a catcher. Just when I thought Betty was running out of objects to throw, I heard Harry shout, "Not the trophy!"

Betty simply wasn't paying any attention to what Harry had said. Just as I peeked over the back of the sofa, Betty threw the trophy at him. Fortunately it wasn't her fastball. It was sort of a change up pitch, something Harry could catch. And now, with the trophy tucked safely under his arm like a football, Harry said, "Let's get outta' here, Jimmy."

We spent the night at the Desert Inn – me, Harry and the trophy. I figured he would want to talk about the incident, but he really didn't. Outside of reminding me that he was a drinker and Betty was a drunk, our conversation was mainly about golf.

During the course of dinner, I mentioned to Harry that I had a golf tournament in Elko next week. It was a Pro-Am tournament with a few celebrities, local celebrities. I was just making small talk, but a second later, Harry invited himself to the tournament.

Harry James would really give my tournament some name recognition. But I honestly felt that Harry had a major problem – Betty. I didn't think she was enamored over the fact that Harry had played in his last tournament, and God only knew what her reaction would be when Harry told her about my tournament.

"Don't worry about Betty," Harry said. "In the morning, we'll stop by the house, get our clubs, and I'll tell her about your tournament."

That's right, I told myself. My clubs are still on Harry's golf cart. Now I knew we both had a problem – Betty.

In the morning we went back to Harry's place to get the clubs and tell Betty about the tournament. I mean to say, I was going to get my clubs and then Harry was going to tell Betty about the tournament.

With my clubs safely on the front porch, I followed Harry into the rec room. It looked like a war zone. But right in the middle of it all was Betty. She was peacefully asleep on the sofa.

Harry kissed her on the cheek. A moment later she looked up and said, "Oh, you're home. How'd the tournament go?"

Talk about a one hundred and eighty degree turn... well, Betty had done that and then some. She had forgotten about last night and her no-hit shut out.

Harry showed her the trophy, and told her he won first place. Then he introduced me. Sure, I was prepared to duck, but nothing happened. There were no cuss words, no guttural sounds, no flying objects, only a wonderful Betty Grable.

But when Harry said, "Oh, by the way," I stepped back and waited for the explosion. I knew what was coming. I knew Harry was going to tell Betty about Elko and my tournament.

"Elko?" Betty asked as she looked at me. "I never heard of it."

With Harry leaving home for a month – the tournament in Elko and a three-week engagement in Reno, he decided to load up the car and drive. And as farfetched as it might sound, Betty helped him pack. What a difference a day meant.

Harry said he would meet Betty in Reno, kissed her good-bye and we took off. No one said a word for about the first thirty miles. Then Harry broke the silence.

"So, what do you think, Jimmy... if Betty wasn't an actress could have she made it pitching in the majors?"

I started to laugh and so did Harry.

"Yeah," I said, "she had good heat on the bottle of bourbon, and her slider with the ashtray looked as though it could hit the outside corner every time. But that knuckler she threw with the trophy was the best one of all."

"It was at that, Jimmy boy," Harry said as he patted the trophy which was safely on the seat between us. "It was at that."

The marriage of Harry James and Betty Grable lasted for twenty-two years. And for twenty-two years, Harry once confessed, he was always the trumpeter and golfer, but Betty was the actress and pitcher.

In my younger days, I played baseball, basketball and football. At the time, I thought golf was a game for sissies.

3

Golf Was A
Game For Sissies

Harry was driving a straight and steady course toward Elko as I sat back and began thinking about the direction my life was traveling. There were many ways to describe my journey through life, but straight and steady was not one of them.

On the contrary, my life was more of an up and down, twist and turn kind of a trip. It just seemed that no matter how well I planned my immediate and long-term future, something always happened to alter the course. No matter what objective I set my sights on, somehow, the fork in the path of life would always take me in a different direction.

In the beginning, everything got started on a rather even keel. I was born in Pocatello, Idaho, and my arrival into the world was, I am told, rather uneventful. And I guess uneventful would be the way to describe the first three or four years of life. But then, around the age of five or six, I saw the first hint that my life would not always go according to plans.

You see, even though I was a mere child, I knew exactly what I wanted to be. It happened one day when I saw an old Hop-along Cassidy movie. After watching Hoppy deal with the criminal elements of his day, I knew I wanted to follow in his footsteps. I wanted to be a cowboy.

Knowing full well I would most certainly spend the rest of my life beating up and shooting bad guys, I got a holster and cap gun. I began practicing the fast draw and pistol whip techniques. My friends didn't mind me practicing the fast draw on them, but no one would stand still long enough for me to develop the art of pistol whipping. Still, my future was a certainty. I would be a cowboy.

Then one day, I suddenly found myself on a different trail. I didn't know how I got there, but I knew that being a cowboy wasn't in my future. Instead of chasing bad guys across the wild west, I wanted to be a fireman.

This sudden career change happened as I watched the town fire truck

Me at the age of four. I want to be a cowboy. No, I want to be a fireman. No... oh, I'll think of something.

race toward a burning building. Wow! I thought. This was spectacular. I can't be certain, but whatever the reason, the red color of the truck, the clanging bell or siren, I knew I wanted to be a fireman. Maybe my friends were still goofing off playing cowboys and indians, but I had set my sights on a career as a firefighter.

In order to get the feel of the business, I hung out at the fire station for a while. The firemen were nice guys, their dog was cute, but nothing ever happened. Before long, I sort of became the firemen's step-and-fetch. This career of fighting fires wasn't much fun. It reminded me of work.

Okay, I ran around town doing a few odds and ends for the firemen only because I knew when the alarm did sound, they would let me ring the siren all the way to the fire. Well, maybe not the siren, but at least, they would let me clang the bell. Siren or bell, it was all the same to me because it meant I would finally get to ride on the fire truck.

My fireman's career lasted five, maybe six days when I began to suspect the fire-fighting business wasn't all it was cracked up to be. Most of my friends were busy playing baseball, while others were starting to play doctor with girls. And where was I? Hanging out at the fire station with a bunch of old men and dogs. And when the alarm finally did sound, instead of getting to ride on the truck and clang the bell, one of the firemen told me to "get the &%#* outta the way, kid." Something was wrong.

After being subjected to that kind of treatment, I just didn't think there was much of a future at the fire station. And since most of the boys, at least most of the boys my age, knew that playing doctor with girls was sissy stuff, that left baseball. I would become a baseball player.

Over the next few years, I enjoyed the game of baseball, but that's not to say I didn't get around to doing a little research in the medical field. Playing doctor was, to say the least, a very interesting and educational

At 12, I was practicing medicine without a license. I was known as Dr. Chenoweth to the girls.

game. Even though I dabbled as a doctor whenever I could, baseball would most definitely be my future. Make no mistake about it, I was a very good athlete, an athlete who participated in all sports. But baseball was truly my game. "One day," I promised myself, "I'll play major league baseball."

In the meantime, to earn a little spending money – very little money at that – I would ride my bike to Ross Park and caddie. At 25¢ a bag, plus a 10¢ tip if no balls were lost during the round of golf, I wasn't going to get rich. But it was a nice way of passing time until the Yankees or one of the other major league teams called.

Being a really smart kid, it didn't take me very long to become an experienced caddie. And as an experienced caddie, I learned there were several things to avoid. I'm talking about hacks, cheapskates and the golfers with heavy bags.

Of course, it didn't take much seasoning to recognize a heavy bag. In fact, the first time I saw Mr. Hilliard show up at the course, I knew his bag was a "no no."

Mr. Hilliard's bag was leather, real leather. And the bag was big, really big. I didn't have to carry Mr. Hilliard's bag to know it was a heavy, heavy bag. But lucky me.

"Jimmy," Mr. Hilliard said as he spotted me crouching down, attempting to hide behind several of the caddies, "you're just the kind of lad I need to carry my bag. You're big, strong and have muscles. Get the bag and let's go."

Struggling to the first tee with the bag I told myself this was going to be a big tip. After all, Mr. Hilliard was the town banker. He was rich. Extremely wealthy. He had to be worth a billion dollars because on the second tee I heard him tell one of his playing partners that he made $10,000 a year. I didn't know there was that much money in the world.

With the round of golf over, I never did receive the large tip I had anticipated. But I did learn a new word. "Economical," the head pro said as I related my horror story about an encounter with a monstrous bag and the non-tipping billionaire. "Don't take it so hard, Jimmy," the head pro continued. "Mr. Hilliard is simply an economical man."

Economical. Conservative. Frugal. Prudent. Thrifty. Yes, I guess there were a lot of diplomatic ways to say it, but sorting out the cheapskates was a matter of experience. Once or twice around the course with a non-tipper, or even a hack for that matter, was all the experience I needed. And for the record, little Jimmy Chenoweth never again broke his back carrying a heavy bag. In fact, my specialty quickly became small bags and scratch golfers who liked to tip.

My favorite person during those days was Fred Huth. Fred had a small bag, was a scratch golfer and owned a chain of drive-in restaurants... successful drive-in restaurants. Fred was a snappy dresser, a big tipper and a great golf instructor.

During a round of golf, Fred would try to teach me the finer points of the game. Fred would say, "Pay attention, because I'm going to show you how to hook a ball." Or Fred would say, "Now watch, Jimmy, because I'm going to show you how to fade a ball."

So, Fred would hook the ball or fade the ball and I would stand there daydreaming about baseballs and stethoscopes. But one day I made an amazing discovery. If I pretended to be really interested in what Fred was talking about, I'd receive a bigger tip.

Immediately thereafter, Fred came to discover that he and I had something in common – our profound love for the game of golf. Fred called me a "real aficionado" and I agreed even though, at the time, I didn't know what kind of fish he was talking about.

Needless to say, Fred and I became real pals on the golf course. He'd tell me things about the game and swing and I'd pretend I was really interested. It got to where I even started asking questions about the game. They were just sort of pretend questions, questions designed to make Fred believe I found the game of golf absolutely fascinating and exciting.

Nothing could be further from the truth, but of course, I never told Fred what I really thought about the game of golf. It was just that every normal healthy boy my age who ever swung a baseball bat or used a garage as an operating room, knew that if there wasn't such a thing called tennis, then golf would be the number one way to waste time. Golf wasn't even a sport. It was a game. And when it came to games, I'd have to rate playing jacks and hopscotch less of a sissy game than golf. I was an athlete, a baseball player. Come on, deep down inside everyone had to know golf was a game for sissies.

Still, I had to admit, there was something about that little white ball and bashing it with a club. And Fred really had a way of making the game sound like fun. But I would never risk my stud status by telling any of my friends those kind of things. As far as my friends were concerned, I earned a little extra money by carrying golf bags for dorks and geeks and sissies.

I do believe, however, that some of my baseball buddies looked at me with suspicious eyes every Monday. It just happened that Mondays were caddie day and caddie day meant free golf for caddies. It was actually a perk, but I told my friends it was a day when caddies were expected to practice their caddie skills. I made it sound as though caddie day was mandatory – everyone had to be there or else.

I lived this double life for nearly ten years. But then, after all those years of refining my baseball talents on the sandlots around town, and those mandatory Mondays at the golf course, I decided it was time for Yogi to move over. In other words, I was ready for the big leagues.

Calvin Walker, a shortstop on the baseball team, and I, hitchhiked to Grand Junction, Colorado, for a tryout with the Cincinnati Reds. I spent three days proving to the Cincinnati Reds that I was a terrific catcher.

Actually, the scouts liked what they saw, but I didn't receive a contract. Instead, I was told to finish school and then the Reds would sign me. I assumed that meant not only high school, but college, too.

Once again, I carefully planned my immediate and long-term future, but this time I wasn't talking about being a cowboy or a fireman. I wanted to play baseball.

The first phase of my plan was to finish high school. And, I'm happy to report that graduating from high school went according to schedule. Then came college. By enrolling at Idaho Southern (now called Idaho State), I felt that after my four years of athletics and a little academics, I would be ready for the Cincinnati Reds. But so typical of my younger days, I found several forks in the road which always seemed to carry me in a direction opposite my objective.

I saw her at a party and she immediately became one of those twists in the road of life. Actually, Betty was more than just a twist in the road of life. She became a detour, a wonderful detour which would last for thirty-three years.

Betty was a cheerleader at Idaho Southern, a beautiful cheerleader. When I saw her that night at a party, it was love at first sight. She was a walking dream come true, the type of woman I could spend the rest of my life with. Except for that little thing on her arm, Betty was absolutely perfect. But... I had seen many girls come to a party with their boyfriends draped on their arms, only to leave with a stud athlete like me. So, getting rid of Betty's little boyfriend and taking her out dancing certainly wasn't going to present much of a problem.

"Why don't you get rid of that thing on your arm and let's you and me cut out of here," I said while approaching Betty.

"Get lost," were the first words I ever heard my walking angel speak. And then, if that wasn't enough, she continued, "Just because you play baseball doesn't mean every girl is going to be there when you snap your fingers. Get lost."

Normally, that wouldn't be the way to start off a relationship. But, I wasn't going to let our first meeting discourage me. I knew what I wanted, and three months later, on New Year's Day, Betty and I were married.

Marriage and the responsibilities that came with it shortened my college

My wife of 33 years and my best friend, Betty.

career. Instead of hitting the books, I was hitting the pavement in search of a job. The only experience I had was baseball. And when the Cincinnati Reds didn't keep a very accurate record of my tryout in Grand Junction, I had to opt for the Pioneer League. So instead of making big money in Cincinnati as a member of the Reds, I was in Idaho Falls playing for a team named after a potato, the Russets.

Johnny Babich, an old-time, semi-famous baseball name for trivia buffs, was managing the Russets. And Johnny said something to me that no one else had ever said, "You ain't no catcher, Jim. You're a pitcher."

Boy, I didn't know about pitching. I felt I was more of a catcher. But when Johnny told me I would be earning a hefty three hundred dollars a month, I started to like the idea of pitching.

At the time, three hundred dollars a month put me way up the pay scale as far as Russets went. And then, as a pitcher, I'd work every three or four days. Big money? A light work load? Okay, I was a pitcher.

Everything in my life was going along rather nicely. I wasn't getting rich, but Betty and I and Kris managed. Kris? Oh yeah, Kris was our first little baby. A cute little baby girl. While looking at my newly born daughter, I promised myself that after one good year as a pitcher for the team named after a potato, I'd become a Giant or a Dodger or even a Yankee. One year and then it would be the majors.

Now in order to grasp the next few paragraphs of my story, a person has to understand that Johnny Babich enjoyed adult beverages. And where I would spend my free time at the golf course playing that sissy game, Johnny would spend a considerable amount of his free time at the local watering hole. One day, just as I was teeing off on a the hole closest to the highway, Johnny drove by. Since Johnny's car was pointed in a homeward direction, I knew he was feeling no pain.

Johnny pulled over to the side of the road, stopped the car, blew the horn and shouted a greeting. Well, I thought it was a greeting.

I hit a perfect drive down the middle of the fairway and waved. But Johnny blew the horn again and this time I realized he wasn't shouting a friendly "hello."

As I approached the car, Johnny screamed, "What are you trying to do, ruin your batting average swingin' a golf club? You'll never be a hitter in the majors swingin' a golf club and playin' that sissy game."

Ruin my batting average? I couldn't ruin my batting average. My batting average was hovering around .050. I think I was something like one hit in twenty at bat, and that hit was an accidental bunt.

"Mr. Babich, I'm Jim Chenoweth. One of your pitchers," I tried to explain as I leaned in toward the window of his car. "My only hit was that accidental bunt."

It was whiskey breath and a man who didn't want to hear any of my lame excuses. From that distant shore where Johnny was looking back into a hazy and blurred world, I was still a catcher who was ruining his batting average by partaking of a sissy game. Without any further ado, Johnny promptly fined me $200.00.

Naturally I felt that with tomorrow being a game day, Johnny would be back to his old normal and sober self. Furthermore, he most likely would have forgotten about the fine and I would, once again, be his strong-armed pitcher with the pathetic batting average.

And I was nearly 100 percent right. The next day Johnny came to work stone cold sober and I was his strong-armed pitcher with the pathetic batting average. But he remembered our roadside encounter and still fined me two thirds of my monthly salary. It was a steep price to pay, especially when a person considers I had a wife and little baby to support.

I liked baseball and still had a passionate dream of playing in the majors, but, I also enjoyed a round of golf. However, with Johnny driving by the course to and from his favorite watering hole, I was faced with a dilemma. I couldn't afford any more of Johnny's two hundred dollar fines for ruining my batting average, and I didn't want to quit golfing on my free time.

Shortly after I paid my fine, Johnny helped me work everything out. It all started during an afternoon game. Even though I tired a little in the later innings, Johnny let me complete the first game of a double header. Wow! I was really on! My breaking ball was hitting nothing but the corners of the plate and my fast ball was blowing by hitters before they had a chance to react. I threw a three-hitter and had a dozen or so strike outs. For the night cap I was ready to sit back and watch my teammates go for the sweep. But once again it was a man who didn't want to hear any of my lame excuses.

Unfortunately, we had a little time to kill between games and Johnny felt he needed some refreshments. When Johnny returned to the ball park, it was obvious he had left something at the old watering hole. I'm talking about his sobriety and his memory. A tipsy Johnny forgot to bring his memory back to the ball park.

Slurring his words a little, Johnny set the starting lineup for the second game. He said, "Chenoweth, you're pitching."

I tried to tell Johnny that I had pitched the first game. It would be pure insanity for me to throw in the night cap. Seriously, what manager in his right mind would use a star pitcher like me in both games?

But I had a major problem getting through to Johnny. He didn't remember that we had played the first game. So, my argument about pitching the first game didn't carry much weight with Johnny. He simply shrugged his shoulder and said something about golf making a sissy out of me.

I didn't care what kind of a name Johnny was calling me. I wasn't going to pitch under any circumstance and that was final. Well... I thought it was final.

"You'll pitch or else I'll fine you!"

Johnny's last statement struck a nerve. Vividly, I remembered my last fine and how difficult it was to survive that particular month. I didn't think my family could outlast another month of fines.

But I was a man and not a mouse. So I did the manly thing. I called Johnny a lot of names... under my breath, of course. And when I was finished with the name calling, I went out and pitched.

During the first inning my elbow and shoulder began to tighten up, but I survived.Between innings I tried to keep my arm warm. However, the temperature was dropping and the Russets only spent money on absolute necessities. Warm-up jackets were not on the absolute necessity list so I had to grin and bear it.

Oh, I could tell Johnny I was cold and my arm was stiff, but I didn't want to be accused of being a sissy. Knowing Johnny the way I knew Johnny, I'm sure he would have blamed my stiff arm on that sissy game. And with just the mention of that other game, Johnny would probably drop another fine on me. No, I told myself, just keep your mouth shut and pitch.

At the start of the fourth inning, I found myself facing a three and two count. The catcher signaled for a fast ball and I agreed. Reaching back to bring a little extra heat, I let one fly. And fly it did.

To this day I still maintain the pitch was a little high. Yes, it was a little higher than the backstop and somewhat higher than the grandstands behind the plate. I can't say for sure if the ball landed in the parking lot or if it's still going because my immediate attention was focused on my arm.

I'm sure it all had to do with the excruciating pain registering in every fiber of my brain, but I could have sworn my arm, wrist and hand separated at the elbow and landed halfway to home plate. Even to this day, it's all sort of blurred, but for some reason I have this memory of me picking up my arm, putting it in my glove and walking into the dugout

Duke Sims, an old friend and former catcher for the Chicago Cubs. He made it, I didn't.

where Johnny attempted to glue it back on.

After that everything was a blank and remained a blank until the doctors removed the cast from my elbow and explained the reason for all the stitches and the nine inch-scar I carry to the day. I'm not saying I lost my arm in a literal sense, but I never pitched again.

My professional baseball career, like those childhood dreams of one day becoming a cowboy or fireman, blew by as reality beckoned. Ah yes, there they were, the three girls in my life looking at my nine-inch scar of one fast ball too many.

Three girls? Did I forget to mention my baby Jan? Well, yes, there were three girls in my life, Betty, Kris and my little baby Jan. And, with a growing family to support I decided to go into the oil business.

I got a job pumping gas at a Standard Oil Station in Pocatello. And in order to subsidize that minimum wage, minimum hour job, I secured employment in the ever-growing adult beverage industry. Pumping gas and tending bar wasn't a bad way to spent a life, but I still had a passion for golf. Time permitting I would take out my clubs and practice. The only problem was that I didn't have a lot of free time for the game I was starting to love.

I had just about given up on a golfing career when the phone rang. "Jim Chenoweth?" a burly voice asked.

"Yes," I answered.

"This is Ted Longworth. I understand you want to be a pro golfer."

"Yes," I replied even though I didn't know who Ted Longworth was.

"Well then, be at Waverley Country Club in Portland by this coming Saturday and you've got the job."

A day later, I learned an old golfing buddy, Cliff Whittle, knew Ted. And when Ted said that Waverley Country Club would be hiring an assistant pro, Cliff mentioned my name. Furthermore, I learned that Ted Longworth, formerly a good ol' Texas boy, was instrumental in developing the careers of Ben Hogan and Byron Nelson. Waverley Country Club sounded like the opportunity I had been hoping for.

When I told Betty about Waverley she said, "The squirrels have got to love you because you're nuts!"

I had the feeling Betty didn't want to pack up and leave Pocatello at the time. But, having a way with words, I turned on my powers of persuasion. I told Betty what a wonderful life awaited us in Portland. Without question it was one of my finest jobs of salesmanship, but Betty was still a tad reluctant as she said, "The day you leave for Portland, is the day I file for a divorce."

Since I didn't think Betty was serious about filing for a divorce, I decided to make the trip to Portland and check everything out. After all, Hogan and Nelson passed through Waverley on their way to the PGA tour. And after his automobile accident, Hogan returned to Waverley and rehabilitated himself under the watchful eye of Ted Longworth. Seriously, not only was this one of the most prestigious jobs in the country, it was my ticket to the big time.

With fifty dollars in my pocket, I bid my family good-bye, climbed aboard the train and left for my great adventure. As the train rumbled over the rails, I went to sleep dreaming about what awaited me in Portland. And what a wonderful dream it was. I'm talking about a band and a group of people, wonderful people waiting for me at the train station. It was sunshine and smiling faces, people shaking my hand and patting me on the back. Then there was Ted Longworth, a kind-looking gentleman waiting for me with open arms. And then in my vision, my dream, I heard Ted say, "Nelson, Hogan and Chenoweth. Now, my trinity of golf is complete."

Suddenly everything was gone as my eyes snapped open to the reality of the conductor shaking me and waking me from this most wonderful dream. I had arrived.

Stepping off the train with my golf bag draped over my shoulder, a suitcase in hand, and big drops of rain splattering against my head, I quickly discovered the band wasn't there. Okay, I told myself, no music, but surely they must be here. I'm talking about the smiling and happy faces from the Waverley greeting committee. But not a single member showed up to welcome the new assistant pro. And hey, what about Ted Longworth? Where was Ted?

Well, I told myself, with the rain and bad weather, Ted is probably running a little late.

After twenty or thirty minutes of standing in the rain, I figured out that Ted was probably running more than a little late. A voice inside of my shivering body whispered the truth. Ted wasn't coming to greet me. No one was coming to greet me.

After a thirty-dollar cab ride, I finally arrived at Waverley. But in miraculous fashion, as we pulled up to the club house, I saw a giant rainbow arc across the sky with its pot of gold located just beyond the tree-lined golf course. It was a sign from God. My new career was about to begin. The storm had passed. The sun was shining. It was a new day.

They were real nice people, but no one in the pro shop seemed to know who I was or why I was there. One of the assistants did tell me that Ted had just left for the driving range. He was giving a member a lesson. So, I picked up my golf bag and suitcase and headed toward the range.

I found Ted sitting on a bar stool watching an elderly man swing a club. Ted was an imposing physical specimen, something of a John Wayne character complete with a large cigar held firmly in his mouth. He was a large man, standing well over six feet tall. He worn a dark golfing jacket, a white shirt and tie.

Since Ted was giving the gentleman a lesson, I sat quietly and watched the master work. This, I told myself, was the man who breathed the breath of life into the careers of Hogan and Nelson. This undoubtedly would be a lesson to watch.

The old man was having a heck of a time trying to advance the golf ball. He was really hacking up the range, but Ted never said a word. He just sat there watching and every so often he grunted.

Finally, after about ten minutes of watching the old man rip up the range, Ted spoke. "Joe," he said in his burly voice. "I've figured out exactly what you need to do."

The old gentlemen stopped swinging the club, turned, and looked at Ted with a trace of excitement on his face. "You really think you can help me, Ted?"

"I don't think, I know I can help you," Ted answered in a positive tone.

"I know exactly what your game needs."

I was really impressed. After watching the old man attempt to hit a golf ball, I honestly thought he was beyond all help. But Ted Longworth, the master, knew exactly what the old man's game needed. I waited for Ted to speak.

Ted slid off the bar stool and said. "Joe, I think you should take two weeks off and then quit the game."

Without saying another word Ted started walking back toward the clubhouse. I stood there as his shadow passed over me. For several moments, I was speechless. Finally I gathered the courage to speak. "Mr. Longworth," I said.

Ted stopped and looked at me. "What do you want?" He asked in a gruff voice.

"Well... Ah... you see," I stammered.

"Out with it boy. I don't have all day here. Now what the *&%$ do you want?"

"Well, I'm Jim Chenoweth."

"So."

"Jim Chenoweth from Pocatello."

Ted thought for a moment, then turned and started to walk away as he said, "Never heard of you."

"No, no, you don't understand, Mr. Longworth. I'm the Jim Chenoweth you hired the other day. Remember? Cliff Whittle told you about me. You called and told me to be here by Saturday if I wanted the job."

Ted stopped in his tracks, turned and looked back at me. "Well what the $&#% are you doing standing out here? You're supposed to be working. Now go on, get over to the pro shop and get to work."

There was no training period, no time to adjust to the job. I went to the pro shop and got to work. And work I did. Sure, I had come to Waverley for a job, but I was also looking to advance my golf career. But the only thing I did was work and work. I spent most of my day working in the pro shop. And then during my free time, I filled the Coke machines, cleaned clubs and sucked up to members. Sucking up to the members was a part of the job. In fact, sucking up to members at any country club is a part of the job.

After working at Waverley for several months, I gathered the courage to face Ted and ask him about my golfing career. Carefully wording and rehearsing what to say and how to say it, I approached Ted after hours in his office. This was the time of day when Ted would sit back and drink a little vodka to relax.

"Mr. Longworth," I said while knocking on the open door to his office. "Can we talk?"

Ted invited me in and we had a rather nice conversation. I carefully explained my interests were in a golfing career and not catering to the whims and woes of stuffy members. However, since arriving at Waverley, I hadn't picked up a club other than to clean it. And I was cleaning everyones' clubs except mine.

"I've been here for several months Mr. Longworth, and I haven't set foot on the driving range one time or even looked at a practice ball."

"Well," Ted said. "We'll have to do something about that."

When I arrived at work the next day for the afternoon shift, my little talk with Ted must have done some good. As I walked into the pro shop, one of the assistants said that Ted was at the driving range and he wanted to see me.

Dusting off my clubs, I picked up the bag and ran to the driving range. I found Ted at the far end of the range hitting some chip shots. "Mr. Longworth," I spoke with obvious excitement in my voice. "They said you were waiting for me at the range. I got here as quick as I could."

"Ah, yes, Jim." Mr. Longworth said as he put his arm around me. "I got to thinking about our talk last night and you were right. You haven't spent any time on the range. So... here's what I want you to do. Every day at noon, I want you to come out here and pick the range."

In my excited condition I thought Ted said for me to come out to the range and practice everyday at noon. But when he told me how important it was to keep the balls clean, I realized my time on the range would not be spent hitting balls but rather picking up the balls.

Shortly after my promotion to driving range picker, Ted and I began to have after-hours conversations in his office. He would take a little drink of vodka and light up one of his big cigars. After blowing several smoke rings and watching them vanish into the air, he would start with stories of Hogan and Nelson and Texas golf. Under Ted's rough exterior, I found a warm, charming and knowledgeable individual. It soon became obvious to me exactly why Hogan and Nelson spent time with Ted. He knew the game but had a simple yet profound way of explaining it.

One evening, while Ted and I were sitting in his office talking about golf, he changed the subject on me. He started asking questions about my wife and children. Ted asked if I missed my family.

I had been away from home for over three months. It seemed longer. Yes, I missed my wife and children. I missed them very much.

Ted looked at me with an all-knowing expression on his face. "That's what I thought," he said. "I sort of figured you must be missing your family. In the morning, when you come to work, there's something I want to show you."

Arriving at work a little earlier than usual, I found Ted in his office. I reminded him about our recent conversation. He remembered. "Come on, follow me and I'll show you what I have in mind."

At first, I thought Ted was taking me to his home. He lived near the golf course and that was the direction we started walking. But then he stopped in front of a cottage next to his place and said, "Here."

Ted handed me a key and two one hundred dollar bills. I wasn't sure what Ted had on his mind. Maybe he wanted me to buy some paint and clean up the place. I didn't understand.

"It's you new home," he said in his typical gruff voice. "I think it's time you brought your family to Waverley, and then we'll see about getting you some range balls to hit."

I was surprised, shocked. There were times when I wasn't sure if Ted even knew my name. But now, here I was, holding the key to the home right next to Ted's. Things were looking up.

As I stood there glassy-eyed looking at the house, I remembered what my wife said when I first mentioned Waverley. Betty said, "The squirrels have got to love you because you're nuts."

And there they were... squirrels everywhere. There were squirrels running on the ground, climbing in the trees and several had established residency in the house. I guess that's why folks around Waverley called this place The Squirrel House. But with a little paint, some cleaning and an understanding between me and the squirrels as to who would live in the house and what would live in the trees, I was positive, The Squirrel House minus the squirrels would become a perfect fit for my family. And it was.

Once my family arrived at Waverley, Ted, in his callous and yet wonderful way, began opening up. Aside from the living quarters which turned out to be terrific, Ted gave me range privileges. It was difficult to believe, but after being at Waverley for only three or four months, Ted finally let me hit the balls I had become so good at picking up and cleaning. And furthermore, Ted started working with me. In his own unique and direct approach to the game of golf, Ted taught me the proper mechanics of the swing.

As an instructor, Ted was way ahead of his time. He was the prototype of the modern golfer and a master at teaching less hands and more leg and hip movement. Under Ted's tutelage I picked up distance off the tee along with accuracy. Before long, I was not only beating Ted on a regular basis, but I was playing in regional tournaments and winning my share. At the time, I really believed I was following in the footsteps of Hogan and Nelson. With my game improving to the point where I was shooting more sub-par rounds than over-par rounds of golf, I told myself it wasn't that far from Waverley to Augusta.

As the crow flies, it was only a couple of thousand miles from Waverley to Augusta. But typical of my life, I went north before I started east.

The Dalles was a club located eighty miles north of Waverley. When I heard about the opening at The Dalles, I sent off my resume and was quickly hired. As the head pro of The Dalles, I would have more time to practice and perfect my game so that when I did arrive at Augusta, the rolling fairways and fast greens wouldn't be a problem.

I expected a lighter work load at The Dalles, but found myself over-whelmed. Something was wrong. Instead of practicing and playing golf, I was always working. This wasn't the way to get to Augusta.

The weeks quickly turned into months and four years later, I still hadn't taken my first step toward Georgia. I needed a job with less of a work load and more time to practice. Someone said, "Ruby View Golf Course in Elko, Nevada, is looking for a head pro. There can't be that many golfers in Elko. I'll bet that would be an easy job."

I took the job at Ruby View and here I was, several years later, coming home after winning a "Big Tournament." It wasn't exactly the green jacket and the Masters, but by Harry James' account, we had just won something bigger than the Masters – the Pro-Am in Scottsdale.

To be honest, by that time in my life, I had pretty much given up the dream of ever playing on the PGA Tour. The lifestyle of tour players wasn't something I relished. Playing on tour meant I would have to be away from my family for long periods of time. I didn't like being away from my wife and three daughters. Betty didn't like me being away either.

Me, Julie, Jan and Kris - my lovely daughters.

Three children? Yes, I now had three little girls. Julie arrived in the world during my stint at Ruby View. Shortly after my little Julie was born, I knew my family needed me more than I needed to walk the fairways of Augusta. So, instead of the pressure of having to make a ten-foot putt on a Sunday afternoon in order to feed and clothe my children, I chose Ruby View.

Maybe I wasn't going to win the four majors, but golf could still become my ticket to a better lifestyle for my family. While playing Pro-Ams in Palm Springs and Las Vegas, I came to realize that celebrities were really getting into the game of golf. It seemed that just about everyone in the entertainment industry was an avid golfer and the fans enjoyed watching their favorite stars on the links. Furthermore, professional golf was becoming popular with a vast television audience. People actually sat in front of their TVs and watched golf. So, I asked myself, why not combine celebrities and golf and TV?

Harry and I were several miles outside of Elko when I began to explain my idea for a television show, *Swing With The Stars*. Harry listened as I detailed the show and the reasons it would work.

"Can't you see it Harry," I said with enthusiasm oozing from every word, "the television cameras are there while Bob Hope and Bing Crosby play a round of golf. They play for pride but the ultimate winner is their favorite charity."

Harry never took his eyes off the road, but I could tell he was doing some serious thinking about my brilliant idea. Finally, Harry said, "It won't work. Bob and Bing..."

I quickly interrupted, "What do you mean it won't work? Golf is fast becoming one of the most popular sports in the country. And people love Bob Hope and Bing Crosby. It will work!"

"I'm not disputing what you've said about golf, TV and the fact that people love Bob and Bing. It's just that Bob and Bing don't love each other," Harry explained. "Not anymore. It will never work. You'd never be able to get them on the same course at the same time."

I didn't understand and so, Harry continued. "Several years ago, Bob and Bing were playing a little golf. It was a two dollar nassau. Bob won the front. Bing won the back and overall. So, Bob owed Bing two bucks. He welched on the bet and Bing never forgot"

Then, without any hesitation, Harry stopped talking about Bob and Bing and started talking about *Swing With The Stars*. And as we pulled into the parking lot at Ruby View Golf Course, Harry said, "I think you've got something, Jimmy. I think we can really make it work."

Harry was right. I did have something. And unlike my early dreams of being a cowboy or a fireman or a baseball player or even a touring pro winning at Augusta, this one would eventually pay dividends... big dividends.

I will always treasure every round of golf I played with the legendary Bing Crosby. He truly was world-class.

4

Swinging With
The Stars

Although Harry James liked the concept of *Swing With The Stars*, he just didn't think Ruby View Golf Course or Elko, Nevada, was the place to get started.

"Jimmy," Harry said, "If we were havin' a rattlesnake round-up, Elko would be the place to have it. But... it's gonna be pretty tough to do any swinging with stars way out here. And then, there's that thing about the government testing atomic bombs out here. All that radiation is bad you know. We need to get closer to Vegas for your idea to work."

Closer to Vegas? I asked myself the question. Maybe Harry didn't understand, but Vegas was closer to where the government was testing atomic bombs than Elko – hundreds of miles closer. But still, I wasn't going to argue with Harry about making a change. In fact, I had been interviewed for the job at Brookside Golf Course in Reno. It looked as though we would be moving... again.

Several months later, I was established in Reno, but Harry James was much too busy to help out. I understood. So, I went to Channel 4 TV in Reno, talked to Director of Sports, Ted Dawson, about my idea, and that was it. We agreed on the name *Swinging With The Stars*, and changed the theme a little. Instead of two celebrities playing a round of golf, I would, once a week, on live television, give a thirty-minute golf lesson to a celebrity. Several weeks later, Pat Boone and I kicked off the first program.

I had never been in front of a camera before, but Pat Boone, the old pro that he was, made everything easy. Pat was so natural in front of the camera that he gave me a comfort level I didn't think was possible. I never experienced any nervousness. We talked about the golf swing, hit some shots, and for all intent and purpose, I did what I had done every day for the last fifteen years. I gave Pat a lesson.

The show worked and once a week I gave another televised lesson to a celebrity. And with Reno being something of an entertainment hot spot, the celebrities were simply a phone call away. It was good exposure for everyone concerned.

The second or third week of the show, Jimmy Dean was my guest. Jimmy was a slicer, a big slicer. "Left to right," Jimmy said. "My ball always goes left to right. I'd give anything to be able to hook one a little."

"Don't worry, Jimmy," I said with complete confidence, "I'll be able to teach you how to hook the ball in no time at all."

With the camera rolling I explained exactly how to hook the ball. That was the first part of the lesson. The second part of the lesson would involve direction. As a slicer Jimmy Dean always aimed left of target. But if he was going to hook the ball, and I was certain he would be able to hook the ball, he would have to aim right of target. However, before I could get into the second phase of the lesson, Jimmy got excited about the prospects of hooking the ball. Before I knew it, Jimmy took a swing and really hooked one.

Unfortunate for the people playing the eighteenth hole at Brookside, Jimmy aimed left of target and the ball went left of where he was aiming. Now I've seen people get hit with a golf ball before, but this guy was really putting on a show. I think the television camera and Jimmy Dean's wallet had something to do with the scene that followed.

There was no doubt the ball did hit the guy, but it wasn't a lethal blow by any stretch of imagination. It was a soft ball. But all of a sudden I

Here I am with Jimmy Dean, one of the funniest and smartest men I know. Let me tell you a story. One day, Jimmy Dean got fed up with flat, flavorless sausage that shrunk up to nothing, so he started his own sausage company. It's as simple as that.

heard agonizing screams and claims of serious injury. Then came the cussing and threat of a law suit. Oh my god, I was only a couple of weeks into my new career and it was already over. And worst of all, the guy was going to sue Jimmy.

But Jimmy had a way with people. Before long, the victim of Jimmy's errant golf ball admitted it wasn't that hard of a shot. Then Jimmy laughed and said, "And getting hit in the butt is the best place to get hit if a guy has to get hit."

Everyone was laughing and when the man agreed to drop any threat of a law suit, Jimmy compted him for dinner and a show at the casino. My career had survived.

Don Adams, aka Maxwell Smart said, "No Jim, that's not a phone ringing, it's my shoe."

Jimmy Rodgers was one of the better golfers I worked with – very talented with a club. This man never complained, you could often hear him say, "It's a darn good life."

In the weeks that followed my guests included Don Adams of *Get Smart*, singers Jimmy Rodgers and Vic Damone, and comedian Norm Crosby.

Don Adams, Jimmy Rodgers and Vic Damone were fairly normal shows. It was questions and answers and a little about shot making. But Norm Crosby was really something. He would ask a question or make a statement as only Norm could. He spoke English and I always thought I knew what he was trying to say. But for some reason I would end up on

Norm Crosby said that he wanted to edit my book. I said "No thanks!"

the ground laughing. Of those early shows, I think Norm Crosby, more than anyone, helped set the tone for *Swinging With The Stars*.

Norm and I were having fun, a lot of fun. And that's what the game of golf should be about. But more important, aside from the entertainment factors, the show was also educational. The celebrities, as well as my home audience, were beginning to understand that golf was actually a very simple game if we didn't let it get too complicated.

Swinging With The Stars soon became a must with any entertainer playing the casinos of Reno. Instead of going out and looking for celebrities to be on the show, they were calling me.

One day the phone rang and it was Milton Berle. He was working in Lake Tahoe and said that he had heard about me from a number of our mutual friends. Milton also mentioned *Swinging With The Stars,* and said that he wanted to do the show. But first, Milton insisted that I go up to Lake Tahoe and give him a private lesson.

Milton said, "I'm putting like a touring pro but can't seem to get the ball airborne or make it go forward."

I thought Milton was exaggerating on all accounts. Most touring pros are deadly with the putter. Some touring pros are better than others, but a person doesn't play on tour unless they can putt. So, naturally I thought Milton was overstating his abilities with the putter. And the other thing I thought was probably just a figure of speech was when Milton said he couldn't get the ball airborne or make it go forward. Come on, anyone can get the ball airborne and make it go forward.

To my astonishment, Milton was a putter personified. He was probably better than most touring pros. I don't know what it was, but Milton Berle could flat-out putt. Long putts, short putts, Milton knew how to get the ball in the hole.

Okay, Milton was a better putter than what he had originally stated, but he was very accurate in his assessment of ball striking. Milton couldn't get the ball airborne or make it go forward. During my fifteen years of teaching, I had never seen anything quite like it.

The first thing I had to do was get Milton a set of real clubs. Milton's bag was filled with woods. That's right... nothing but woods – no irons.

With the right mixture of clubs, you know, irons and woods, Milton's game quickly began to improve. The ball went up in the air and in the general direction he was aiming. Thinking he was on the right track, I said, "Now, Milton, all you have to do is practice."

I don't know if it was his busy schedule or something else, but Milton never practiced. He just never went to the range and hit balls. Milton loved to play, but never spent any time working on his game.

Still, after several lessons, and Milton always insisting he wanted to do my show, I scheduled him. He came to Reno, and with live television being live television, I didn't know what to expect. But then again, Milton Berle owned live television.

To no one's surprise Milton was a little nervous before we went on the air. After all, the show was about hitting a golf ball and not cracking a joke. But once the camera started rolling, I couldn't believe the change that swept over Milton. The nervousness was gone and he performed as though he was born with a golf club in his hand. I had given Milton lessons and played a number of rounds with him, but when he did *Swinging With The Stars,* he was never better.

From that beginning, Milton and I went on to become great friends. I found Milton to be a solid guy, a terrific human being who was always trying to help people achieve their goals. I guess that's why he took an active interest in *Swinging With The Stars.* He wanted to see me succeed in a world beyond Reno.

"Jim," I heard Milton's familiar voice over the telephone, "I know your show is doing well in Reno, but I think it's worthy of more, much more."

Milton then told me that he had contacted Danny Thomas Productions and mentioned *Swinging With The Stars.* Milton said, "Danny thinks that if you went back to your original idea of having two celebrities play a round of golf, and make charity the big winner, the show could be a hit on national television."

I took the next flight to Los Angeles and a day later, Milton and I drove over to Danny Thomas Productions. We had a meeting with Danny and his nephew and producer, Ronald Jacobs.

The first meeting went quite well. We talked about the popularity of golf, and began putting together an outline of how things would work. When the meeting was over, we shook hands and agreed to meet again. Everything sounded like a go.

Milton was so positive that *Swinging With The Stars* was going on national television that he drove me across town to his voice instructor. Milton felt if I was going to be working on a big time television show, I should know the proper way of projecting my voice.

After my voice lesson, I left Los Angeles and during the next several weeks met with Ronald Jacobs up in Reno. We were getting along just fine and I expected contracts to be forthcoming.

Several more weeks went by and I hadn't received the contracts. However, there was no question in my mind that we were going to do the show. So, I started talking to my friends in the business, the entertainers originally connected with my Reno version of *Swinging With The Stars.*

Then I received the phone call from a friend in Los Angeles who told me the news. Yes, Danny Thomas Productions was doing the show, but I was out and Lee Trevino was in. I couldn't believe what I was hearing, but Danny Thomas Productions was about to begin filming its new show, *Swinging With The Stars,* featuring Lee Trevino.

I called Danny Thomas, but the secretary told me he was busy. I called Ronald Jacobs, but he was busy too. I made several more phone calls to Danny Thomas Productions but everyone was busy.

Yeah, they were so busy that no one returned my calls.

Well... Milton Berle did return my phone call and he couldn't believe what I was telling him. He said there had to be a mistake. "Jim," Milton said, "I've known Danny a long time. This couldn't be happening."

However, when Milton checked everything out, it was happening. It wasn't a mistake. Danny Thomas Productions was shooting a program called *Swinging With The Stars*, and I was the odd man out. But there was a reason, of course. Someone at Danny Thomas Productions told Milton I was "unheralded... everyone knew Lee Trevino."

I know Danny Thomas did a lot wonderful things during his time on earth. In fact, Danny Thomas' story of how he founded Saint Jude's Children Research Hospital in Memphis, Tennessee, proved he had a lot of depth and compassion. And I for one am thrilled Saint Jude's can provide hope to so many little children who otherwise would be looking at a bleak future. However, I never met the Danny Thomas who founded Saint Jude's. I met a different person, a person who approached business with a cut-throat attitude.

My business association with Danny Thomas ended when I had to get a court injunction to stop him from using the name, *Swinging With The Stars*, for the program his company was already filming. Unfortunately I couldn't stop him from doing the show because he had altered the format a little. But I did what I could and then I brushed the dust from my sandals and moved on.

At the time, Jimmy Dean's son, Robert, was working for me at Brookside. Naturally, it didn't take very long for Jimmy to find out what had happened with Danny Thomas Productions. Jimmy called me and when I gave his the details, he was extremely upset. He promised he would do something to help me. But what could he do?

Several weeks later, Jimmy called back and told me to get on the next plane to New York. He had scheduled a meeting with Loren Hassen of Harbinger Productions. Loren was the producer of Shell's Wonderful World of Golf and American Sportsman. He was interested in *Swinging With The Stars*.

I was surprised that Jimmy Dean was able to come through for me especially in light of Danny Thomas' debacle, *Golf For Swingers*. Danny's show bombed after only two or three weeks. But fortunately for me,

Jimmy Dean became a real friend to me, my wife and family. He was very instrumental in getting "Swinging With The Stars" off the ground and was a very positive influence to me and my family.

Danny had radically altered my original idea so much that I couldn't take any credit or blame for his production. Evidently, Danny thought he needed some girls with tight-fitting outfits and a lot of joking around to make the show work.

Well... the bottom line was that Danny's show didn't work and I was off and running with one of my own.

From the very beginning, Loren Hassen and I hit it off. He was direct and right to the point, a no-nonsense type of a man. His plan was to do a pilot show and take it to an agency which represented Toyota. Loren felt that with Toyota sponsoring the show we would be guaranteed at least one year on national television.

With contracts signed, we were scheduled to shoot the pilot show in Reno. Dale Robertson was hired to do the commentary, I would provide the analysis and color, and actor David Wayne would square off against Bing Crosby for the actual match. But, the day before the cameras started rolling, it snowed. That seemed to be the story of my life. Nothing ever came easy. So, we packed up the production company and moved to Scottsdale, Arizona.

The weather in Arizona was perfect. A high pressure system was hanging over the desert and the weatherman said there would be nothing but sunshine for the next week. Still, I wasn't going to take any chances. I helped the boys unload the equipment and even helped them set up for a practice shoot. Since I was a little familiar with Bing's game, I walked the nine holes with the director. We were just trying to put the cameras in positions where we could really focus on Bing.

For example, Bing wasn't a long hitter but very straight. So, we would mark off spots on the fairway where I thought Bing would hit his drive and work from those points. Then, at exactly three in the afternoon, I watched as he pulled up in a golf cart. Punctuality was one of his traits. He was wearing the familiar hat and with a pipe held firm between his teeth, he introduced himself to the Director and crew. "Hi, fellas, I'm

Bing Crosby."

Bing played a few holes so that everyone would get the feel of the shoot. Then he said, "I think we all have it down pat, so why don't you fellas go on and cut out of here. I want to play a few holes with Jim."

The director was satisfied everything would work, and the crew was happy to call it an early day. And as for me... well, I always enjoyed a round of golf with Bing. We played until the sun went down. As a matter of fact, we played two holes in the dark. Bing had that kind of a game. He'd swing the club and two hundred yards down the middle of the fairway he would find his ball day or night. He had that kind of a game – not long, but accurate.

This was a very exciting time in my career. My first "Swinging With The Stars" show starred Bing Crosby. What a thrill! Shown above, David Wayne, Bing Crosby, me and Dale Robertson on the set, November 1971.

Afterwards, Bing and I went out for dinner. We talked about golf and the mechanics of the game. Then we discussed the many mutual friends we had. It was a good evening and I had to asked Bing about Bob Hope. After all, Harry James said that Bing and Bob really didn't get along.

Easing into the conversation, I mentioned that I had played in the Bob Hope Desert Classic and didn't see him there. "I was surprised, Bing. I figured that you'd play in Bob's tournament and Bob would play in yours."

Bing sat back in his chair and said, "No, Jim... I don't play in Bob's tournament and he doesn't play in mine. As a matter of fact, we don't play much golf any more."

I mentioned what Harry had said about the bet. Bing smiled and replied, "Harry James really gets around, doesn't he?"

"Yeah, he does at that," I said.

Then Bing looked me in the eye and said, "Harry's right. Bob doesn't pay his bets. So, I don't golf with him any more."

With our pilot in the can, Loren Hassen took it to the Clinton E. Frank Agency. A week later, Toyota called and wanted to meet with me and my attorney, Frank Fahrenkopf in Los Angeles. Everything sounded good, but I was still a little uptight. I wouldn't rest until the contract was signed.

We met a group of Japanese businessmen representing Toyota in the offices of the Clinton E. Frank Agency. They watched the pilot show three, maybe four times. Then they had a little powwow. Obviously, something was wrong. I started to get the feeling that maybe I was born with a dark cloud hanging over my head and it was always raining.

Finally, one of the Japanese businessmen said, "We like the show very much except for one thing. Dale Robertson looks good on a horse. But Dale Robertson does not look right on a golf course."

Instead of canning the show, Toyota wanted to drop one cowboy, Dale Robertson, and pick up a former Dallas Cowboy quarterback, Don Meredith. And to my surprise, both cowboys were amenable to the move. Don Meredith was interested in doing the show, and Dale

Robertson received a nice check and rode off into the sunset.

The only thing that remained was drawing up the contract, signing it and getting started. And of course, until they completed the paper work, I would be a little nervous. I didn't want anything to go wrong. I wanted it to work. Several weeks later, I received the phone call. The contract was ready.

My attorney and I flew back to Los Angeles and headed straight for the offices of the Clinton E. Frank Agency. But during the flight, I kept thinking that maybe a stray missile from one of the air bases around L.A. would down our flight. And once we were safe on the ground, I kept thinking about an earthquake hitting while we were jammed in traffic under one of the freeway bridges. But there were no missiles and no earthquake. Finally, I saw the parking lot of the office complex.

Upon our arrival, a very nice receptionist asked us to be seated in the outer office. She went behind closed doors, obviously to tell the boss we had arrived. I was just about ready to breathe a sigh of relief when it started – the commotions. I heard someone yell, "I think he's having a heart attack!"

Then another voice shouted, "Quick, call a doctor!"

"A heart attack!" I said to my attorney. "Did I hear them say he was having a heart attack?"

Before my question could be answered, I heard a third voice from behind the closed door, a quieting voice say, "No... he's not having a heart attack."

I crossed my fingers and hoped for the best.

Then the third voice continued, "No, no, he's not having a heart attack. He's already had the heart attack. Call the coroner... He's dead."

The boss, whatever his name was, had a heart attack and died with my contract clutched firmly in his hand. The only thing I remember is peeking into the office and seeing a man face down on his desk with the contract in hand. After that it all became a blur and when my eyes focused again, we were on the plane jetting back toward Reno.

I knew that life was full of ups and downs, but this time I was all the way down. It was so bad that I was feeling sorry for myself. I guess the thing that troubled me the most wasn't what had happened in Los Angeles, but what would happen in Reno when I had to tell my wife that our dreams of a new and better lifestyle for the children were nothing more than smoldering ashes.

The flight attendant interrupted my painful thoughts when she asked, "Would you like something to drink and a bag of peanuts?"

"No... no drink or peanuts," I answered. "Just open the door so that I can jump."

The flight attendant laughed. She must have thought I was joking. I assured her I wasn't.

Then she said, "Come on now, it can't be that bad."

"It's worse than bad," I said.

Since there was only a few passengers on the flight, she sat down and we talked. I told her the whole story... everything. I told her about Danny Thomas and how Jimmy Dean came in and saved the day. I told her about filming the show in the desert with Bing Crosby and coming a heartbeat away from signing the contract.

I thought my sad story was really getting to the flight attendant because she reached out and gently touched my hand. It made me feel good, almost as though I had a friend helping me through the darkness. Then she looked into my tear-stained eyes and asked, "Do you really know Jimmy Dean?"

"Well... yeah, I know Jimmy," I answered even though her question came as a surprise. I really expected her to say something comforting... You know, some words of encouragement, something to get me through this crisis in my life.

"Wow... I can't believe it. You really know Jimmy Dean."

Suddenly my problem became secondary. At least the flight attendant viewed it that way. She started asking Jimmy Dean questions and I started answering.

She asked, "How does Jimmy treat his fans and people in general?"

"I was in a grocery store with Jimmy one day when a little old lady asked for his autograph. While he was signing the little lady's autograph, other people recognized him. Before long, there was a line of Jimmy Dean fans waiting for their autograph. We must have spent an hour there... me watching and Jimmy signing."

The more questions I answered about Jimmy Dean, the further I seemed to distance myself from one of the most devastating days in my life. It was a form of therapy, reminiscing, talking about an old friend.

"Jimmy's boat," I found myself sharing memories with the flight attendant, "he named it, *Big Bad John.*" And with that I talked about my wife and me spending a wonderful two weeks with Jimmy on the boat. We cruised the waters off the Florida coast. It was a memory I will cherish forever.

One of the other passengers interrupted my trip back through memories. He wanted a drink and some peanuts. The flight attendant said, "I'll be right back."

I looked out the window and saw the landscape below, a dark landscape dotted with sporadic lights from passing cities. It was a pretty scene – peaceful and beautiful. Then I passed a thought about the many people living down there, living in that arena of ups and downs. Only then did I realize life was the same for everyone. We all win some and lose some and tomorrow is another day.

A second later, I felt someone tap me on the shoulder. I turned and saw that the flight attendant was back. Sitting down in the seat next to me she asked, "And you really know Bing Crosby, too?"

"Yeah," I answered, "I know Bing Crosby, too."

Without giving her a chance to ask another question, I thought it was the right time to tell her one of my favorite Bing Crosby stories. It happened one day when Bing called with a question about golf.

I was having a bad day, a real bad day. Instead of answering Bing's question, I started unloading on him. Before long, I was telling him all of my troubles, my worries and woes. He listened and when I was finished, he told me a story.

Bing spoke in a voice that could only be described as Bing Crosby. You know what I mean, a smooth voice, kind and gentle.

Bing said, "You remind me of an old friend of mine, Jim, a friend that was given a heavy cross to carry through life. One day it got so bad that my friend couldn't go on. He got down on his hands and knees and begged God to take back the cross and give him a smaller one.

"Suddenly, my friend was transported to a place beyond earth and time. He entered a large room, a room filled with crosses of all sizes and shapes. Then my friend heard a voice, no doubt the voice of God. And the Voice told him to look around and pick out the cross he wanted... any cross. Well, my friend did exactly that. He looked around and saw an assortment of crosses. There were big crosses, smaller crosses, heavy crosses, crosses which reached to the ceiling of the room and crosses with rough, wooden splinters. It was a difficult decision, finding the cross he would want to carry for the rest of his life. But finally, my friend looked in the corner of the room and saw the perfect cross. It was a small cross made from smooth wood.

"Lord," my friend called out. "This is the cross I want. Please, Lord, if I have to carry a cross through life, let me carry this one."

"But," the Voice spoke, "that is the cross you brought into the room."

The flight attendant gently touched me on the hand and whispered, "How much I envy you. Not because you know Jimmy Dean and Bing Crosby, but because you have some wonderful friends."

"That I do."

I taught several golf clinics at Bally's casino in Reno, Nevada, where I was Executive Director of Golf from 1986-1990.

5

From Tee To Green
To Hollywood

I guess the one interesting and unique thing which separates me from the average person is the people I've met along the way. Of course I'm talking about individuals from the motion picture community as well as entertainers in general. You know the kind of people I'm talking about... those individuals who have reached for the stars and gained celebrity status.

Typical of anyone who ever watched a movie or sat marveling at an entertainer or even laughing at a comedian, I formed an image of that person. If they were tough guys on the silver screen, I could picture them walking through real life as tough guys. And of course, good guys in the movies had to be good guys in real life, and the virgin queens of Hollywood productions were virgin queens in the everyday world. Yeah, sure.

When it comes to the world of entertainment I think we're all a little naive, perhaps even gullible. Sometimes we fail to realize that an actor is an actor, an actress an actress, an entertainer an entertainer and a comedian a comedian. When our favorite stars are away from the spotlight, some of them are a lot different from public perception.

Take Jerry Lewis for example. Before I met Jerry, I expected him to be the guy we saw in the movies and on television. Don't we all have an image of Jerry being something of a half-baked clown, stumbling along, and tripping over his own feet?

Why there was a time when I thought Jerry was the most ungainly, clumsiest, awkward guy on the planet. Even if I gave Jerry the benefit of doubt, I would have still bet the house that he was a little uncoordinated. Acting was acting, but no one was that good an actor. Jerry Lewis, I was sure, had two left feet.

Boy, was I wrong about that one. Let me be perfectly clear about this because Jerry Lewis was a tremendous athlete. He had the best eye-hand coordination I had ever seen. Jerry was balance, grace and poise. In fact, I think if Jerry had worked at it, he could have become a great golfer. He was simply that good an athlete.

Then there was Buddy Hackett, another guy who could go out on stage and make people laugh. I got the impression Buddy was a cuddly, fun-loving type of a guy. I even pictured Buddy out in my back yard playing with the kids and making them laugh. But then one day I played a round of golf with Buddy. I walked away from that experience just shaking my head back and forth.

You see, in real life, it always seemed to me that Buddy Hackett tried a little too hard to be funny. By going to these extremes to get a laugh, Buddy would ultimately come across as a little strange.

Okay, we've all seen some strange things happen in life and especially on the golf course. But one day, during a round of golf at Brentwood Country Club, Buddy Hackett took strange to a new level.

Jan Murray, Buddy Lester, a comedian friend of mine, Buddy Hackett and I were playing a rather normal round of golf. Hit the ball and move on to the next shot. Hit the ball and move on to the next shot. Then Buddy Hackett hooked one into the heavy brush. I'm talking about huge green leaves, trees, branches, weeds... you know, something of an African jungle.

The foliage was so thick, I thought Buddy would just let the ball go. I certainly wasn't going to help him find his ball. And Jan and Buddy Lester

Golfing buddy and funny man, Jan Murray.

had no intentions of crawling into that patch of wilderness and looking for a two-bit ball. This was Southern California, a section of the country known for rattlesnakes and other types of varmints that bite.

Buddy said, "My ball's in there."

"Yep, Buddy," I said, "*your* ball is in there."

"Ain't you guys gonna help me find it?" He asked.

The three of us answered in unison, "Not me."

Suddenly, Buddy got down on all four and plowed ahead into the thicket. In a matter of moments his chubby little backside vanished into the heavy green leaves. He was gone.

"He's nuts," I said to Jan and Buddy Lester. "board-certified nuts!"

I think he expected us to laugh. But no one was laughing because it was funny and yet it wasn't funny. It was, like I said, "Nuts."

Suddenly, we heard Buddy start to scream and yell. "A hairy thing gots me! HELP! A hairy thing gots me!"

It sure sounded as though something did get Buddy. Wow... There was a lot of screaming and yelling coming from the brush. But... if it was a wild animal, I thought, surely we would hear the growling or the animal making some type of noise. Aside from Buddy's screams and the noise of him thrashing about in the foliage, there was no sound of a wild animal. It was rather obvious that Buddy was putting on some kind of a show. But instead of his audience laughing, everyone was stunned.

The screaming went on for several minutes, several boring minutes. Then we realized Buddy was trying to bait us... play a joke on us. He must have thought that if he screamed and yelled long enough, we would dive into the bush to save him. Save him from what, I asked?

"Come on, Buddy," Jan shouted into the brush. "Let's go! We're backing up the course."

We were backing up the course. And even the other people playing adjacent holes were starting to look at us in a strange way. Hey, this was a country club, a prestigious country club, but Buddy kept screaming and yelling and begging us to save him from "this hairy thing."

Finally, when Buddy realized no one was going into the brush to save him, we saw the leaves swaying back and forth as he crawled out of the wilderness. But hey, something was different. I had to rub my eyes just to be sure I was seeing what I thought I was seeing. But there could be no doubt about it, Buddy Hackett was missing most of his clothes. His shirt was gone, his pants were undone and down to his ankles, and a shoe was missing.

"Geez, fellas," he said while brushing leaves and branches from his hair, "a bear attacked me and you guys wouldn't help."

Funny? Hell yeah. But it was funny in a strange kind of a way. Of course, we laughed, but at the same time, I thought it was a long and dangerous road to travel just for a laugh. So, that's what I mean when I say Buddy was a little strange.

Now if a person was interested in taking the meaning of strange to a lower level, all they had to do was get invited to a Hollywood party where anything goes. I had heard rumors about wild parties in Beverly Hills, but for the longest time that's all I thought they were – rumors. Then one night Billy Eckstine, the great black singer, invited me to a big-time Hollywood producer's home for Martha Raye's birthday party.

Billy said, "I'm going to show you a side of Hollywood you never saw and I think you'll get a kick out of these goin' ons."

Great singer, great golfer and great friend, Billy Eckstine.

Nearing the home... ah... I mean the palace, I could hear blaring loud music and raucous laughter along with some squealing... high-pitched squealing. Damn! I even heard something that sounded like someone making that Tarzan sound. You know, the noise Tarzan made while swinging through the vines.

Circling the block while looking for a parking space, Billy smiled and said, "Sounds like the place is really jumping."

Well, the place was not only jumping, but crowded. Why it was so crowded, we had to park a block away. Then, as we started walking toward the palace I began to understand what Billy meant when he originally said, "I think you'll get a kick out of these goin' ons."

As we began walking up the driveway to the palace, I heard someone screaming. It was coming from a nearby parked car. It was a woman's voice! She was really screaming! Blood-curdling screams! My god, I thought, she was being murdered!

I'm really not the hero type, but there was no doubt in my mind that this woman had to be fighting for her life. I would never forgive myself if I didn't help a lady in distress.

I ran to the car, and pulled open the door. I looked in. There was a guy on top of a lady. Just as I was ready to yell at the guy to get off the lady, he looked up at me. Then the lady looked up at me. Ah... she wasn't being murdered.

"Ooops," I said. "I guess this isn't my car after all."

I gently closed the car door and continued up the driveway with Billy. And once again the woman started screaming. "Well," I said to Billy, "it does sound like she's being murdered. Doesn't it?"

We entered the palatial estate and instantly I came to understand that in the matter of wild Hollywood parties, rumor had substance. This was one of those wild Hollywood parties most of us country bumpkins only hear about.

The first thing I think I saw was another murder being committed about halfway up the spiral staircase. If this guy and gal weren't wearing skin tight, pink suits, then they were naked.

Not one to stare, I looked away only to see the revival of the Roman Empire. I was mesmerized. Speechless. It was not a sight for the squeamish. It wasn't even a sight for the stout of heart. This was hedonism.

"Billy," I had to ask. "Is this some kind of a nudist camp?"

"No." Billy answered as he nonchalantly took a drink from the tray a butler was carrying. "Why do you ask?"

"Well, I don't know if you've noticed, but outside of the butler, we're the only other people wearing clothes."

With that Billy woke up and took a good look around. For several moments he too was speechless. Finally he said, "This is a little more than I expected, Jim."

If it was more than what Billy had expected, imagine what a kid like me was thinking. Heck, I was from Reno by way of Elko. In Reno, unlike some other areas of Nevada, prostitution wasn't even legal. And in Elko, we had our share of legal "ranches." But everyone knew only "ladies" worked there.

However, this wasn't Reno and it was a far cry from Elko. This was a big-time Hollywood party and it was way beyond anything I had ever seen. It was further south than even my most perverted thoughts. Not even my wildest imagination could have ever taken me to this world.

Oh, sure, I read in a history book where big-time parties brought the Roman Empire to its knees. And the Good Book mentioned that God nuked Sodom and Gomorrah for similar conduct.

Sodom and Gomorrah, I thought as I watched the "goin' ons." Boy oh boy, if God nuked Sodom and Gomorrah for conduct unbecoming humankind, then there was a very good chance some incoming missiles were heading for this place.

Just as I was ready to suggest to Billy that we leave, I saw the birthday girl, Martha Raye. She was standing in the middle of the ball room, making guttural sounds with a group of guys around her. And when I say I saw Martha Raye, I mean I saw Martha Raye.

Once again I was ready to suggest that we leave when some old guy, wearing only a loin cloth, jumped from a table, grabbed on the chandelier and started swinging back and forth. It was incredible. Unbelievable! I had to ask. "Billy, who did you say that was swinging from the chandelier?"

No sooner had I asked the question, the old man started the Tarzan cry. With that I recognized him.

"Oh, that's Johnny Weissmuller," Billy said. "I've seen him do that before. He's always trying to convince these producers that he still has another Tarzan movie or two left in him."

Yeah sure, I thought. I can see it now. Johnny Weissmuller as Tarzan. Martha Raye as Jane, and that's the day the audience starts rooting for the alligators.

"Jim," Billy tugged on my sleeve while staring in disbelief at the party, "I think we've seen enough."

Fifteen minutes later, Billy and I were at an all-night driving range near Studio City. We hit balls into the wee hours of the night. We had a good time. But we kept looking toward the dark sky over Beverly Hills expecting to see the bolt of fire and mushroom cloud.

Most of my stories about celebrities are mild by comparison to my one and only big-time Hollywood party. In fact, during my golfing seminars I often tell celebrity stories to a mixed audience of young and old alike. You see, most of it is strictly PG. They are the kind of stories that people enjoy hearing and I enjoy telling. And here are a few of my favorite ones.

George Burns On Living To Be
One Hundred Years Old

To my knowledge George Burns was not a golfer even though he spent a considerable amount of time at Hillcrest Country Club in Los Angeles. Now George may have picked up a club when I wasn't around, but I never saw him actually hit a golf ball or even walk out on the course. In fact, the only times I saw or talked to George was when he would come into the club for lunch. And that, I've been told by the regulars, was just about every day.

Hillcrest Country Club had a place of honor, a big round table where the legends and only legends of the entertainment industry would sit. The table was called, and rightly so, Legends of The Round Table.

Although I wasn't a legend, Milton Berle saw to it that I had the special privilege of occupying a seat at the Round Table. So, whenever I was in Los Angeles, and Milton took me to the club, I got to sit quietly and listen to the legends tell their stories of Hollywood.

While sitting at the Round Table, I got to meet such wonderful stars as Jack Benny, Jan Murray, Jack Lemmon, James Cagney, Edward G. Robinson and many others. But one of my all-time favorite people was George Burns.

I met George Burns in 1976 shortly after his Oscar-winning performance in *The Sunshine Boys*. And even though many, many years have gone by, I can still vividly picture George sitting at the Round Table and speaking in his wonderful, crackling voice.

"Imagine that..." he said. "Me, winning something called Oscar. Even when Gracie and I made films, we weren't what you called an actor and actress. We were vaudeville back then and I'm still vaudeville today."

I never realized it but George Burns had been away from his original film career for thirty-five years. I found it interesting that even though George was away from the business for all of those years, his star never dimmed.

George once told me, "Jim, if you find my career interesting, I find it unbelievable. How can I win an Oscar? Oscar is for people who can act... Movie stars. Gracie and I never made a movie. We did something called 'shorts' – productions that weren't even long enough to be considered movies. And now, I make my first legitimate movie, *The Sunshine Boys*, and I get lucky. Imagine that..."

After several years of bumping into George at the club, we got to know each other fairly well. There were even times when Milton and the boys would go out and play a round of golf, and I'd stay behind just to visit with George. He was an intriguing man, a funny guy, a good person.

Then one day while George and I were sitting at the Round Table, he said, "Jim, I'm gonna tell you the secret of living to be one hundred years old. And just to prove I'm telling you the truth, I'm making plans to be around when they celebrate my one-hundredth birthday. Remember what I'm telling you... one hundred candles... and then after that, I'll go on to be with Gracie."

George called the waiter over and asked for a pencil and paper. When the waiter returned, George slid the pencil and tablet over toward me and said, "If you want to live to be one hundred years old, you better take notes. This is important."

With a pencil in hand, I listened as George began. "The first thing a person has to do, if they're looking for a cake with one hundred candles, is to have a bowl of soup every day. Now I'm just not talking soup," he said. "I'm talking chicken soup and it has to be piping hot. Now write that down – a bowl of chicken soup, every day, and piping hot."

Come to think of it, George did have a bowl of soup every time I saw him at the club. And it was hot! Boiling hot! In fact, it was so hot I always thought he was going to burn his mouth if he wasn't careful.

George patiently waited as I wrote my notes about chicken soup, every day and piping hot.

"Did you get that part about piping hot?" George asked.

"Yes," I answered while reading from my note. "Piping hot."

"Good," he said with an affirmative nod.

Then, George showed me the next ingredient in his "live to be one hundred" theory. And believe me, at the time, that's what I thought it was – a theory. George was already in his early- to mid-eighties. And even though he did get around quite well, I really never expected he would live to see one hundred years.

"Now," George was saying, "you see this?" He showed me a rather long and thick cigar.

"Yes," I answered.

"Well, you've got to smoke fourteen of these every day."

Naturally I had to ask, "Why fourteen?"

George looked at me for a contemplative moment and then answered, "I guess it's because I light up exactly fourteen cigars a day. I light one up, smoke it a little, and put it aside. Then I forget where I put it. So, I start all over. I sat down and figured it all out one time. And fourteen is the exact number of cigars I light up and attempt to smoke every day. Fourteen. So, write that down, Jim – fourteen cigars a day."

George continued, "Now this is really important. After lunch, and the piping hot soup, you've got to go home, drink two martinis and take a good long nap."

With George looking on, I wrote my note – *martinis and a nap.*

George picked up the tablet and glanced over my notes. He was quite serious about this.

"You wrote martinis... add the word two. It's gotta' to be two martinis," George insisted as he slid the tablet back toward me and tapped his finger on the word *martinis.* "Make sure it's two martinis. And then, you wrote *nap.* It's gotta be a long nap. So write the word long in front of nap."

Satisfied my notes were accurate, George continued. "And now, Jim, when you get up from the long nap, you've got to go out on the town and chase after some dollies."

"Dollies?" I asked.

"Girls. Young girls." George explained. "It's important for a guy to stay busy chasin' after the dollies."

"George, I couldn't do something like that. I couldn't go out on the town and pick up young girls. I'm married."

"Jim, I didn't say anything about picking up young girls. I said to chase after the dollies. It's the exercise, Jim. Seriously, at my age, even if I did catch a young dolly, I wouldn't remember what to do. And besides, Gracie would never forgive me."

The thing that really impressed me about George Burns, was his love for his wife of 36 years, Gracie Allen. No matter how many times I talked with George and regardless of which direction our conversations went, he always seemed to work his way back to the subject of Gracie and how much he loved her and how much he missed her.

With it so very obvious that George loved and missed Gracie, one day, as we sat alone at the club, I just had to ask him. "George, every time we sit here and talk like this, it's obvious that you still love and miss Gracie. So, why do you want to live to be a hundred years old?'

"That's a good question, Jim. I told a lot of people the secret of living to be a hundred. But no one has every asked me why? You did, and here's the honest answer. Absence really does make the heart grow fonder. It's the same way on the other side with Gracie. We're just storing up enough love to last for eternity. So, I'm going to live to be a hundred, and then I'll go on to be with Gracie."

I kept those notes for the longest time. And every year on January 20, I'd hear the news – George Burns had another birthday. Finally, in January of 1996, George Burns had his birthday cake with one hundred candles. He made it. He and Gracie had stored up enough love to last for eternity.

When I heard that George passed away shortly after his birthday, I felt as though I had lost a friend. I was sad. But then I remembered what he once said. "Absence really does make the heart grow fonder."

I doubt that I'll live to be 100 years old – the hot soup burned my mouth, I got sick smoking all of those cigars, and even after a long nap, I was still too tired to go out on the town and chase after the young dollies. But as for George Burns, I got a feeling that someday, somewhere, we'll sit down at the Round Table and talk over the old days. In the meantime, every so often, I take a page out of George's notes on living to be one hundred years old. It has to do with the martinis... the two martinis. You see, whenever I feel a little sentimental, I look up at the stars and drink a toast to Gracie Allen and my old friend, George Burns, who not only shared with me his secret of living to be one hundred years old, but also his reason.

Forever, George Burns and his story of living to be one hundred years old will share a special place in my heart. I'm not talking about the piping hot soup, fourteen cigars, the long nap, the two martinis or chasing after the young dollies. It's just that George and I had something in common. George lost Gracie in 1962, and twenty years later, on June 15, I lost my wife of thirty-three years, Betty. Yes, George Burns was right, "absence really does make the heart grow fonder."

###

"You Dirty Rat!"

If a person likes the beauty of falling snow, then Reno, Nevada, in the dead of winter isn't a bad place to visit. But if a person is a golfing buff, then I suggest something a little south of here and at a lower altitude.

It was a typical winter, and by the end of January, I was looking for a way out. So when the phone rang and I heard Milton Berle's voice begging me to come to Southern California I quickly accepted the invitation. Milton said he was making putts from all over the place, but was having a difficult, if not impossible time getting from the tee to the green. I had heard it all before.

"Jim," Milton said, "please... you've got to help me. I can't miss with the putter, but the rest of my clubs are useless. I can't get the ball airborne."

Arriving in Los Angeles, I expected to find the sun shining. It wasn't. A low pressure cell was sitting off the coast and really dumping buckets full of rain on LA. It was depressing. I left home with the expectation of being outdoors and hitting golf balls. But now this – the rain! The monsoons!

Milton's home in Beverly Hills was on secure ground so I didn't have to worry about a mud slide pushing us over a hill and into any of the flooded canyons. All we had to do was sit tight and wait for the storm to pass.

But Milton was Milton and he couldn't wait. He got out some equipment and was ready to start hitting balls in his living room. But his wife, Ruth, put an end to that. Ruth was the boss and no matter what Milton said or did behind her back, her word was final. And I have to admit that every time she turned her back, Milton made a face. And when she left the room, Milton spoke his mind. But in the end, Milton decided to sit tight and wait for the storm to pass.

Well... we sat tight and waited... waited for about thirty seconds when Milton suggested, "Let's go over to the club."

Naturally, Hillcrest Country Club was closed. At least the course was closed, but the clubhouse, for anyone foolish enough to brave the storm, was still open.

Only because Milton insisted, I rode over to the clubhouse with him. I honestly didn't think anyone would be there. The weather was terrible and only a complete fool would venture out on a day like this.

Arriving at the club house, I couldn't believe it. We weren't the only ones out on a day like this. Not only were Edward G. Robinson and James Cagney sitting at the Round Table, but several of the other tables were occupied.

"See," Milton said as we started across the room, "I told you the boys would be here."

As we approached, Edward G. looked up, and with a big cigar dangling out of his mouth he whispered to Cagney, "I told you some knuckle-heads would show up to golf on a day like this."

Of course, Edward G. whispered loud enough for Milton and me and everyone in the room to hear. And of course, Cagney whispered back in the same tone, "It doesn't take much more than an atom of brain to know you can't golf on a day like this. But then again, no one ever said he was the brightest guy in the world."

"Milton," Edward G. said, "we were just talking about you. Have a seat."

Although Cagney and Edward G. were great tough guy actors, I could tell they were tugging on Milton's leg a bit. And what made it funnier was that Milton knew it too.

Here I was, sitting at the Round Table with two of the greatest tough guy actors in the history of motion pictures and they were doing a number on Milton Berle. And Milton was being Milton – nervous, squeamish, and uncertain of himself. We've all seen it many times, Milton Berle, seemingly in over his head but simply playing to the crowd.

Actually, I had met Cagney and Robinson before. During those times we engaged in small talk, conversations about their days before Hollywood.

Both Cagney and Robinson came out of New York's Lower East Side. Cagney, younger than Robinson by six years, was the son of an Irish bartender and a Norwegian mother. He helped to support his family by working as a waiter and poolroom racker.

Emmanuel Goldenberg, on the other hand, had every intention of becoming a rabbi. Then he was going to be an attorney. Then he changed his name to Edward G. Robinson (the G. stood for Goldenberg), and after a 15-year career on Broadway, he became a movie tough guy, a gangster by another name.

I'd guess the job of a poolroom racker helped establish James Cagney as a tough guy. But not many of Cagney's fans know that during the early days of his career, he worked as a female impersonator. Then Cagney joined the chorus of the Broadway production *Pitter-Patter.*

I had been a spectator at the Round Table on several occasions when Edward G. Robinson poked fun of Cagney for his work as a female impersonator. And with Cagney being involved in something called *Pitter-Patter,* Edward G. Robinson, in his best Hollywood tough guy, gangster voice, would suggest that Cagney wasn't such a tough guy after all. He called him a sissy... and worse.

I can still picture Edward G. Robinson sitting at the Round Table and doing his tough guy impersonation of gangster boss Rico Bandello from the movie *Little Caesar.* With Cagney seated to his right, Edward G. said, "I dropped my car keys in the parking lot one day and glanced back to see him standing there." He motioned toward Cagney, and then continued in his dead-serious gangster voice. "I kicked those keys across town to my driveway before I bent over to pick 'em up."

It was hilarious, but don't think for one second that Cagney didn't take his shots at Edward. It was a fairly well-known fact that Edward G. Robinson, the toughest, most forceful, authoritative gangster boss in the history of motion pictures had, in real life taken a serious whipping at the hands of a little gal named Gladys Lloyd.

Gladys was Edward G. Robinson's wife. And, as the story goes, after 29 years of marriage, Gladys decided to end it. And end it she did.

To pay off the divorce settlement, Edward G. Robinson had to sell his art collection. But this wasn't just any art collection. It was reported to be one of the largest privately owned art collections in the world.

So, when Edward would suggest that Cagney was living in a closet, which he wasn't, Cagney would counter by embellishing the "real, behind-the-scenes story of exactly how Gladys slapped Edward all over town until he not only gave up but gave her everything."

"Now you got to understand," Cagney would say with a trace of an Irish accent, "if I hadn't seen it with me own eyes, I would never, not in a million years, have believed it. But there I was, hiding in the corner, when Gladys grabbed him by the collar, bounced him off four walls and the ceiling, and then proceeded to roll up a newspaper and beat him like a dog. It made me cry, to see a grown man beaten like that... a man who has such a reputation for being a tough guy."

Their verbal jousting would usually end with Edward banging his fist down on the table and shouting, "Why you dirty rat!"

Then Cagney would bang his fist down on the table and shout, "Why *you* dirty rat... stealing my lines!"

After calling each other a dirty rat several times over, everyone would laugh, have a drink and go on to the next story.

Usually this type of kidding would only happen if Milton wasn't around. But when Milton was there, both movie tough guys would pick on him instead of each other. And believe me, neither Cagney nor Robinson took prisoners.

So there we were, sitting at the Round Table as the rain flailed the windows while Cagney and Robinson went after Milton. It was good material, exceptionally funny stuff – Cagney and Robinson were playing the part of movie tough guys and Milton was the inept Uncle Miltie.

Milton said something, I don't even remember what it was, but Cagney slammed his fist down on the table and screamed, "Why you dirty mouse!"

Just then, and as if on cue, the waiter appeared with a little plate of cheese for Milton. By now everyone was laughing. But then, suddenly, Cagney and Robinson stopped laughing. They looked toward the doorway. Something or someone had come into the room. And both movie tough men had focused their attention on whoever or whatever was there. Everything was serious now, very serious.

I twisted in my seat and turned around to see what had captured Cagney's and Robinson's attention. And there he was – Jack Benny.

Looking back on that day, I find myself wishing someone was there to have filmed those next several minutes. No one said a word and yet it was one of the funniest things I had ever seen. Cagney and Robinson were glaring at Jack Benny. And they were everything they had even been on the silver screen. Why if looks could kill...

And Jack Benny just stood there, framing the doorway as only Jack Benny could do. It was often said that Benny's successful style of comedy was based on timing and perfect use of the pause for milking laughs. Well, his timing was perfect and his pause was milking laughs. Everyone in the room, except Cagney, Robinson and Berle were laughing.

Yes, even Milton Berle was playing the part of a tough guy, a gangster, a buffoon type of a character.

For the longest time, Benny just stood there with that expression on his face. How does one explain that expression? I can't.

Then Jack folded his arms like he was known to do, and placing his hand and finger against his cheek he spoke. "Why you dirty rats."

Oh my God, I was on the floor. I had heard that line time and time again. But no one in the history of entertainment had ever uttered those words with less emotion or lack of zest than Jack Benny. I was laughing so hard my sides hurt. Everyone was laughing except Jack. He stood there, pausing, milking it for everything it was worth.

Finally, Jack sort of waltzed toward the table and sat down. That's when the fun began. For the time being, Milton was off the hook and Jack Benny was on it. And for the next hour or so, Cagney, Robinson and Berle had a field day at the expense of Jack Benny.

They started out by describing Jack with such words as *thrifty* and *conservative*. The next words I heard were *bargain, economical,* and *inexpensive*. Then Milton blurted out the word *cheap*, and shortly after that all hell broke loose.

Someone must have had a Thesaurus hidden under the table because they used every conceivable word to substantiate that Jack Benny was a little frugal. They called him *miser, stingy, cheapskate, hoarder, money-grabber, scrooge, skinflint, tightwad* and several downright nasty names. But Jack sat there and watched and listened and never said a word.

Finally, after about thirty minutes, they ran out of words to describe Jack's thrifty tendencies. That's when Jack said it again, "Why you dirty rats."

It was funnier the second time around, because Jack said it with less emotion and less zest then he did the first time.

We sat at the Round Table for most of the afternoon drinking and eating. And of course, they were still picking on Jack, especially Milton. But when the rain stopped and the sun broke out, everyone decided it was time to head for home.

I don't remember who called for the tab, but that's when Jack stepped in and said, "Now, once and for all, I'm sick and tired of you guys always accusing me of being a miser, a cheapskate, or a tightwad. So, just to show you I'm not, I insist on signing the tab. And, I'm not going to take no for an answer. I insist."

For several moments no one said a word. They just sat there and stared at Jack.

"Well... someone could have at least argued with me a little bit," Jack said as he picked up the tab and signed it.

Since my seat was right next to Jack's, I had a perfect view of him actually signing the tab: *Milton Berle.*

Then he turned and looked directly at me. And with a wink he said, "Jim, I've never done anything like this before, so you'll have to help me out. What is a normal gratuity, a normal amount to tip? One percent? Two percent? Two and a half percent?"

"For a momentous occasion like this," I answered, "I think you should tip fifteen percent."

Just then Milton, while lighting up a cigar, said, "If it was me, I'd tip twenty percent." He fanned out his match, took a puff on the cigar and repeated, "That's what I'd do... twenty percent."

Jack shrugged his shoulders and said, "Oh, what the hell... since I've never done anything like this before, I'll make it twenty-five percent."

Contrary to popular belief, Jack Benny was not the miser he pretended to be. In fact, in real life, Jack Benny was a very generous man even when he was signing his own name to the tab. But somewhere during his early days in show business, he got a laugh out of pretending to be stingy. And, for the rest of his career, so very typical of Jack Benny, he milked it for all it was worth.

And as for James Cagney and Edward G. Robinson, movie tough guys... well, they had a presence on the big screen and even in real life... when they were seated. But when they stood up and walked away from the Round Table that day, I realize just how tiny in stature they were. Neither man stood much taller than 5 foot 3 or 4, and yet, they were legends, giants on the screen.

###

Lucy, I'm Home . . .

She must have lived within walking distance of Milton Berle's home because she always seemed to be dropping in for a casual visit. I'm talking about Lucille Ball. I'd hear the doorbell ring, and a second later her familiar voice would shout, "Miltie. Ruth. It's me. Anyone home?"

I never saw Lucy arrive at Milton's home in a car, and I never saw her arrive in Milton's home without a drink in her hand. It was that way the first time I saw her, and the last time I saw her. She always had a drink in her hand.

The focus of this little story isn't to suggest that Lucy was a heavy drinker. I don't know if she was or she wasn't. I merely mention the drink in hand because that was the way she would arrive at Milton's home.

The first time she dropped by Milton's place, as I said, I recognized her voice immediately. I thought about everyone's favorite television show, *I Love Lucy.*

However, a second or two later, when I met her, it was a little bit of a shocker to me. She was much different on television playing a part than she was in real life. Much, much different.

The television Lucy, in my estimation, was an adorable conniver, always plotting, always scheming in a cute and hilarious way. I just loved to watch Lucy come up with her hair-brained schemes and then hear, "Lucy, I'm home." It was funny! Good entertainment – Lucy, Ricky, Fred and Ethel.

But the real-life Lucy, I have to admit, was a little hard around the edges, strictly a business woman who knew what she wanted and obviously knew how to get it. Now don't get me wrong because I'm not saying Lucille Ball wasn't fun to be around. She did have a sense of humor. But she was kind of loud and outspoken. She would say exactly what was on her mind and flavor it with some shocking four-letter words.

In fact, when Ruth introduced me to Lucy for the first time as Milton's golfing pro, Lucy said, "Wow! What a &%#$ hunk! What a big %$#& stud! When are you going to come over to my place and give me a golf lesson or two?"

Maybe I'm wrong, but I just couldn't see *I Love Lucy* saying something like that on television. Then again, *I Love Lucy* was make-believe, and the Lucille Ball standing in Milton's living room was the real thing.

It all comes back to what I said in the beginning of this chapter. We watch the entertainers on television and in the movies, and based on those performances, we form our images. Sometimes the television and movie image is true to life, other times it is not. In the case of Lucille Ball, her TV image was radically different from the real Lucille Ball.

Nonetheless, during my first meeting with Lucy, she kept insisting that I give her a lesson. She wanted to learn how to golf.

"I'm serious," Lucy said. "I want you to teach me how to hit that #%$ little white ball. Right now!"

I had been teaching people how to swing a club and golf for most of my adult life, but I couldn't remember anyone asking for a lesson the way Lucy did. She got my attention.

"Well..." I said in kind of a sheepish voice. "I guess we could make some arrangements. You know, get together at a driving range."

"Driving range my &*#$%," Lucy answered. "I want to learn now. Right now! Out in the back yard!"

I had given Milton's son, Billy, a set of Hogan clubs. And whenever I was in town, we would practice some short chip shots in the back yard. Lucy saw the clubs on the patio and that was it. She wanted a lesson.

We went out in the back yard, but it wasn't much of a lesson. I tried to give her some instructions on the chip shot but Lucy kept insisting, "If I was interested in putt-putt golf I'd go to the place where they have that &%$# windmill or Ferris wheel or whatever the &%$# it is. I want to learn how to hit the &%$# ball. Do you understand? HIT that &%#$ little white ball."

Lucy did have a good set of lungs and could really express herself. Furthermore she had a mind of her own. I was saying "chip the ball" and she was shouting "hit the &%$# ball."

Milton lived in a quiet neighborhood, and with the homes rather close, I was sure the folks living on the other side of the hedge could hear the commotion. Heck, the shoppers at the far end of Rodeo Drive could probably hear everything.

"Chip the ball," I'd whisper.

"But I want to learn how to hit the &%$&# ball!" she would shout.

I never did get around to giving Lucy my "chip the ball" lesson, and fortunately she never really did "hit the &%$& ball!" Oh, it wasn't that she didn't try to hit one because she did take a full swing. Fortunately she missed the ball. But the divot, about a three pounder, went over the hedge and into the neighbor's back yard.

When the neighbor shouted, "Chip the &%$# ball!" the lesson was over. At least it was over for the time being.

But now Lucy was insisting that we go to the driving range. "You got me excited about this &%$# game," she said. "And now, I really want to hit the &$%# ball."

Milton and I were scheduled for a match at the club with Jack Lemmon and Fred DeCordova, the producer of the *Johnny Carson Show*. Graciously I attempted to bow out of giving Lucy her lesson. But she wanted to come over to the club for a quick lesson and a round of golf with the boys.

I don't remember exactly how it happened, but I think Milton said he was going to go to the bathroom, and I said something about picking an orange in the back yard. I wasn't even sure Milton had oranges in his back yard. But Milton knew what I meant and I knew what Milton meant. Fortunately, it took Lucy a few minutes to figure everything out.

By the time I crawled through the hedge on the side of Milton's home, he was already in the car with the engine running. I had done a lot of golfing during my life, but this was the very first time I had to escape to the golf course. And escape we did, and not a moment too soon.

Just as I jumped into the car and Milton slammed it into reverse, Lucy came running out of the house, screaming for us to, "Wait!"

Milton said, "Pretend you don't see her."

Pretending that we didn't see her was a real tough thing to do, because when Milton put the car in drive, he nearly ran Lucy over. Hell... she was blocking the road.

Milton made a hard left to avoid hitting Lucy, and then a quick right to miss the on-coming traffic. I looked back over my shoulder, and Lucy was still out in the street watching us drive away.

"Hey, I love Lucy, too," Milton said. "But if we ever took her to the club they'd sure as hell throw me out."

That evening I took a late flight back to Reno. I thought that would be the end of giving Lucy golfing lessons. But when I arrived at home, my wife informed me that Lucille Ball had called. Lucy wanted to make arrangements to bring me to Los Angeles for a series of lessons.

I didn't know what to do. As an instructor, I wanted to help people play better golf. But I wasn't sure Lucy would understand there was a difference between golfing and "hitting the %$#& ball."

Early the next morning, the telephone rang. I answered, and it was Desi Arnaz. You know, the Ricky Ricardo of *I Love Lucy* fame.

"Jim," Desi started the conversation, "I understand you met Lucy yesterday."

"Well... yes, I guess you could say that."

Actually, I had known Desi for several years. We met at the Del Mar Race Track in 1971 or 1972 when I was there with Bing Crosby. Desi had a home down in the Baja and I think he also had another place in Del Mar. At any rate, Desi and I had played a couple of rounds at Tijuana Country Club. I also got together with Desi at Torrey Pines Golf Course in LaJolla, California, and had given him lessons a number of times.

So, I wasn't surprised that Desi was calling, but I was a little taken back that he was talking to me about Lucy. You see, Lucy and Desi were divorced in 1960 and I didn't think they spent much time together anymore.

Desi got to the crux of the matter quickly. He said, "I understand you're gonna give Lucy golf lessons. Do me a favor and *dun't.*"

Desi had a funny way of pronouncing the word *don't*, but I understood. I tried to tell him that I hadn't agreed to give Lucy the lessons. But he wasn't listening to me. He just rambled on.

"Look, Jim.... If you got to give her lessons, then teach her the wrong way to play. Give her bad lessons. Make it hard work. Make her miserable so that she *wun't* want to play."

"Desi," I said. "I couldn't do something like that. I couldn't take money for lessons and then not teach a person how to play the game."

I wasn't telling Desi that I would teach Lucy to golf. I was simply saying that I couldn't take money for a service and not provide the service. But Desi wasn't listening and he interrupted again. And once again he was rambling on. He was telling me that Lucy was a strong-willed woman. He said that she couldn't take no for an answer no matter what. He said that she was loud. He said that when she had a drink or two, she got louder. "Jim," he pleaded. "I still got friends in Los Angeles... friends who golf. I couldn't let Lucy ruin golf in Los Angeles.

And believe me, Jim... if Lucy went out on the golf course she would ruin it for everyone."

I was beginning to understand. Lucy did show up at Milton's house with a drink in her hand. And she did seem a little tipsy. And... she was a little loud... a little too loud for any golf course I had ever played. I had to agree with Desi. The Lucy I saw stopping traffic out in the street in front of Milton's house might wear out a welcome rather quickly on any golf course.

Suddenly I was remembering an old show from *I Love Lucy.* Lucy and Ethel wanted to learn how to golf. Ricky and Fred tried to talk the girls out of golf lessons. When Ricky and Fred couldn't change the girls' minds about taking up the game of golf, they gave them lessons... "Bad lessons" as Ricky would say. They made the game much more difficult than it was – hard work and not much fun. It was a funny show! But this wasn't television.

"Look, Jim," Desi was still rambling on. "Here's what I'm gonna do. When Lucy calls for lessons, tell her you're busy. And then, I'll pay you double for not teaching her how to golf. That way you *dun't* have to teach her bad. Jus' *dun't* teach her."

Once again, I tried to get a word in, but Desi just wouldn't listen. As he continued the one-sided conversation, I understood perfectly his reasoning. He didn't want to see Lucy on the same golf course where his friends might be golfing. Judging from my first meeting with Lucy, I could see where she might disrupt the normal flow of a golf course.

So, I once again attempted to communicate with Desi. I was trying to tell him I understood but he continued on. I held out the phone and let my wife listen. He was speaking English, Spanish, Pig Latin and all three languages at the same time. Finally, Desi thanked me for understanding, for listening, and then bid me good-bye.

Several days later, I received a check from Desi and a little note. He said after thinking everything over, he decided to triple my normal fees for not teaching Lucy.

I never cashed the check and Lucy never called again. Furthermore, even when I was in Los Angeles at Milton's home and Lucy did drop in, she never mentioned golf. Of course, Ruth never introduced me as Milton's golfing pro either. Instead, I was just a good friend of the family.

Interestingly enough, Lucy said I looked familiar. Milton quickly retorted, "Jim's got that kind of a face. He looks a lot like everyone but no one in particular."

Lucy agreed, but I for one didn't know what Milton had just said. I guess it really didn't matter what Milton was trying to say, because at least the golf courses in Los Angeles were safe.

From Eccentric To Weird

Vic Damone was a great entertainer, a first-class guy and a pretty fair golfer. So whenever he would call for lessons, I'd jump at the opportunity. You see, his game never required much more than a little tweaking. And after the lessons and a round of golf, Vic would treat me to dinner and front row seats wherever he was playing. When I say Vic Damone was first-class, I mean exactly that – first-class.

Naturally, when the phone rang and I heard Vic's voice asking if I could schedule him for a lesson, I was on the next flight to Las Vegas. And so typical of Vic, the limo was there at the curb waiting for me.

Usually, the driver would take me over to the Sahara where Vic would be waiting at the driving range. I'd work on his swing for an hour

To the world he is known as Vic Damone. To me he is simply first class!

or so and then we'd try to take everything from the range to the course.

Sometimes it's a lot easier to hit the ball on the range than it is on the course. So, that's why I would like to take everything to the course for a playing lesson. Imagine that, I was getting paid for playing.

However, today was a little different. Vic was waiting for me in the back seat of the limo. And after we exchanged all of our "hellos and how's it going," Vic told me we had a quick stop to make before going to the golf course.

Vic said, "There's this wealthy but eccentric person in town who occasionally requests a private show. He just called... and... well... I don't like to turn him down because he pays a lot of money for a couple of songs. It won't take long... fifteen minutes at the most."

It all seemed innocent enough to me, a wealthy but eccentric guy wanted to hire Vic Damone for a private show. But... there was something about the way Vic said, "wealthy but eccentric," something that begged for the question to be asked.

"Vic," I casually asked, "who are you talking about? Who is this wealthy but eccentric guy?"

Vic mumbled a name. It almost sounded like he said "Howard Hughes."

I laughed and replied, "It almost sounded like you said 'Howard Hughes.'"

"I did."

Chuckling a little I told Vic that I could agree with the "wealthy" part of his statement, but felt using the word "eccentric" to describe Howard Hughes was an exercise in diplomacy.

"No, no," Vic said. "Howard's not that bad."

"Vic," I said, "Howard was eccentric when he built and attempted to fly that big plane – Hercules or the Spruce Goose or whatever it was called. But since then, I've heard he's taken eccentric to a place south of the border called weird."

"No I'm telling you, Howard's not that bad. You know how it is... rumors get started and people stretch everything a little. The last time I saw Howard he wasn't bad.

Well... It was another question just begging to be asked. And so I asked, "When was the last time you saw Howard?"

It turned out Vic hadn't seen Howard for over a year. Perhaps I was wrong, but I had a feeling a lot had happened to Howard Hughes in a year.

Arriving at the Desert Inn, I let Vic know that I would, if possible, be interested in watching his performance. That was just a nice way of saying I wanted to see how far south of the normal and rational border Howard Hughes was actually roaming. And from all the stories I had heard, I was sure old HH was traveling in uncharted territory.

It was said that Howard Hughes had actually started heading south a year or so before he moved into the penthouse suites at the Desert Inn. But in November of 1966, when Howard established residency at the Desert Inn under the cover of darkness and secrecy, the rumor mill really kicked into high gear.

To begin with, November of 1966 was the last time anyone ever saw Howard in public. Folks said he was something of a recluse. And they said his hair grew down to his shoulders and he never washed it. And I heard he never trimmed his fingernails. And there was that little story circulating around about germs and Howard. The germs were out to get Howard. At least that's what Howard thought. So HH started wearing a surgical mask and instead of clothes, he wore a diaper. If Howard Hughes was just ten percent of what rumor had him, then I was very interested in seeing Vic perform. I wanted to get into the room and see Howard Hughes for myself.

It's not that I wanted to make fun of Howard. I guess I could say it was curiosity. I was simply curious to see if there was any substance to rumor. I mean Howard Hughes was worth what? Two and a half billion dollars! At one time he was a Hollywood playboy. And now he had become the man of mystery.

Vic didn't have a problem with me going in to watch the show, but several of Howard's people did. Oh, I got on the private elevator and made it to the main floor of the penthouse, but that, at least for the time being, was the end of the line. Howard's bodyguard opened a door and let Vic pass, but I was told to wait out in the hall.

I called them bodyguards, but stood correct when one of these goons said they were "male nurses – Male Mormon Nurses."

Not one to give up, I continued pleading my case with the Male Mormon Nurses. I told them that I wanted to go in and watch Vic perform. I don't think they believed me. I think they thought I was going to go in and check out their boss.

Several moments later, the elevator doors opened and out stepped Jim Whetten. Originally, Jim was a business man from Utah – auto dealerships, I think. But more important, at the time, Jim was one of HH's most trusted people. He was something like number three or four in command.

I had met Jim at the Desert Inn on several occasions. At first he was surprised to see me. After all, not many visitors came up to the penthouse.

Explaining that I had come over with Vic, I told Jim I wanted to see the show. He looked at me for several moments. I really think he understood what I was saying. And for whatever his reason, he said, "Let him in. Let him sit in the corner by the door."

One of the "Male Mormon Nurses" escorted me into the room, and pointed to a chair in the dark corner. It was kind of spooky, the room that is. But, I did as instructed and sat quietly in the background as my eyes adjusted to the darkness.

Toward the front of the room, I saw a big leather chair with several overhead lights, muted lights sort of outlining the chair. I could also see the outline of Vic sitting in the front of the room patiently waiting.

The other thing I noticed was all the windows were taped over with newspapers. Not even the faintest ray of sunshine could get into the room. I suddenly thought of a vampire. There was no doubt in my mind! This room was not something a living, breathing, human being could enjoy.

Just as I was ready to excuse myself – the show wasn't worth the depression I was feeling – a door opened, and two of the "Male Mormon Nurses" carried Howard into the room and placed him on the leather chair. At least I thought it was Howard Hughes.

If this was Howard Hughes, and I suspected it was, then several malicious rumors about him were quickly laid to rest. Heck, he wasn't wearing a surgical mask. And furthermore, he wasn't wearing a diaper. Where did this surgical mask and diaper nonsense start?

Instead of the surgical mask, Howard was wearing rubber gloves – surgical gloves, I think. And instead of the diaper he was wearing his birthday suit.

Let me explain it this way. If Howard wasn't wearing surgical gloves, then he wouldn't have been wearing a damn thing. I'm talking completely naked.

To tell the truth, I'm not sure if Vic sang or not because I was totally and completely stunned. I would have to believe that the show went on, and it must have been a good one, because Howard sat there very intently watching and eating one Hershey candy bar after the other. Unbelievable!!!

Howard Hughes sitting in a leather chair, with his long hair, a frail naked body, surgical gloves and Hershey candy bars. Now I knew for certain, Howard Hughes was a long, long way from reality.

Vic and I never talked much about the journey from eccentric too weird. And that's because a picture was worth a thousand words. I don't know about Vic, but I sure have a picture of that particular day pressed against the conscious chambers of my mind. It's something, no matter how hard I've tried, I just can't forget.

It's just a side note on Vic Damone, but something worth mentioning. Not only would I come down to Vegas to teach Vic the finer points of the game of golf, but he would also come up the my course, Brookside Golf Club in Reno. I was the Director of Golf at Brookside for a while.

And one day, Vic saw a beautiful young girl working in a restaurant at the club. The girl was not only beautiful to look at, but she was a beautiful person. But she had a little problem – some crooked and chipped teeth. Everyone could tell the girl was self-conscious about her teeth, but Vic was the only person to do something about it.

Vic told me to find out what it would cost to take the girl to a dentist and get her teeth fixed. I did and later told Vic what it would cost – $1,500.00.

Vic simply said, "That's not much money to pay when it's going to give a beautiful person a little self esteem."

With that, Vic Damone opened his wallet and counted out fifteen hundred dollars. So, when I say that Vic Damone is a first-class guy, believe me, Vic Damone is first-class and then some.

###

Joe Louis
& The IRS

I was Director of Golf at the Sahara Hotel in Las Vegas when the brain storm hit me. And what a brainstorm it was... a golf tournament with professional athletes and amateurs. I would bring in, all expenses paid twenty or thirty professional athletes, and then sell a golf and gambling package to the general public. I knew I could pull in some big-time sports figures and the Sahara's mailing list of recent clients had more than enough names to make this one work.

I know everyone in the country is doing the same thing these days – pro-am tournaments which feature sports figures. But, at the time, I was one of the first ones to come up with the idea.

I started planning the tournament and quickly discovered I was absolutely right. Once the sports celebrities found out everything was free, it wasn't hard to bring in the big names. Everyone enjoys a freebie once in a while.

And as for the amateur players... well... one way or another they were going to pay and pay dearly. Of course, everyone wins in Las Vegas.. or at the very least, they all break even. Yeah sure, everyone breaks even and yet Vegas keeps building bigger, better and more expensive casinos.

Break even or win, once I had secured names like Johnny Bench, Whitey Ford, Willie Mays, Rollie Fingers, Dizzy Dean, Rick Barry, Happy Hairston and many others, the tournament sold out. This would be a couple of days of golfing and a few nights of gambling.

The day we were going to play the practice round, while walking from my office toward the course, I saw Joe Louis, former Heavyweight

Willie Mays. Baseball was his game, but he wasn't bad at golf either.

Champion of the World in the parking lot. One of my employees was talking to Joe and when they saw me approaching, the employee said, "Here he comes. This is Mr. Chenoweth."

There was another person with Joe, and they both had golf clubs. I was pretty sure it was Joe Barrow Louis, Jr. But, I hadn't invited Joe or his son to the tournament. I knew Joe was doing PR work for Caesar's Palace, but I forgot to invite him to the tournament.

Well... I figured someone must have invited him without telling me or he heard about the tournament and just showed up. Hey, I wasn't going to tell Joe Louis that he couldn't play in the tournament. I wasn't stupid, if Joe Louis wanted to play in my tournament, then Joe Louis could play in my tournament.

It turned out the other person was his son, Joe Jr., and he was in town for a few days. Joe Jr. was a banker in Denver and he had come to visit his dad. It was a little vacation, a few days away from the grind. So, Joe wanted to know if he and his son could play a round of golf. They didn't even know about the tournament.

At the time, I didn't understand why, but I could sense a real sadness about Joe. Sure he was a gentle person, quiet, almost shy, but the thing I really noticed was a dominating sadness pressed against Joe Louis.

"Certainly," I said. "You and your son are welcome to play the course any time, Joe... anytime. I'm going out right now. Why don't you and your son join me."

Then I mentioned the tournament to Joe and suggested that he and his son play in it. Joe's face really lit up as he said, "I think we'd like something like that. Yeah, we'd really like that."

Joe Louis was a good stick. He hit the ball solid and knew what he was doing. After about six holes Joe asked, "Jim, would you like a little bet?"

Joe and I made a little bet... something like a buck a hole, and I gave him four or five strokes. When our round was over, I was down four dollars. I said, "Don't punch me Joe," and paid him immediately. Joe laughed a little, but it was a quiet laugh.

Golf has a way of breaking down barriers. What I mean to say is that when you play a round of golf with a person, you feel like you get to know that person. And that's the way it was with Joe Louis. I felt as though I knew him, really knew him. And with that, I could sense something was wrong.

I took Joe and his son inside, got them a drink and we talked. During the conversation I became positive something was wrong. And so, after a while, I had to ask. "Joe, it might not be any of my business, but I got a feeling something is bothering you. Is it anything I can help with?"

To my surprise, Joe opened up and explained his problem. He told me he owed back taxes and the IRS was after him. I knew about the taxes. Everyone did. That was the way the IRS worked. They would get a celebrity like a Joe Louis and try to make an example out of him. It wasn't right, it just wasn't right.

"Well," Joe said, "I had a bad morning. They came and took my car. The IRS grabbed my car. Now my son's in town and I don't have a car to take him sightseeing."

There were many thoughts racing through my mind at that moment. I thought about Joe Louis and what he did for our country... what he did for the world when he knocked out that big ugly German in the first round. Joe was an American hero, a hero to all the people of the world who were against Hitler, Nazi Germany and what the *Sig Heil* crowd stood for. Then I thought about Joe joining the Army. And instead of making big money in the ring he went and fought exhibition fights for our troops all over the world. Joe Louis was a good man, a great man, a true American and now the IRS had taken his car because of back taxes. It just wasn't fair.

"Heck Joe," I said while reaching in my pocket for my car keys, "We have two cars. My wife hardly ever uses hers... So here... take mine until you get something to drive."

Joe looked as though I had just paid off his million dollar tax bill. I tried to tell him it wasn't that big of a deal. It was just the loan of a car until he got something to drive. You see, we really did have two cars and my wife hardly ever drove hers. So, it wasn't that big of a deal.

Joe insisted it was a big deal. He kept telling me I was a good man and he would never forget it. And I told Joe he was a great man, and I would never forget what he did for his country and the world. Sure the propaganda machine of Nazi Germany tried to convince the world they were the master race, superior to the rest of us. But it took Joe Louis only one minute to prove Nazi Germany was a lot of BS.

###

Liberace's First
And Last Golf Lesson

He was born Wladziu Valentino Liberace. He'll always be remembered as a flamboyant, elaborately costumed pianist and showman. But for those who marveled at the entertainer and never had the opportunity to meet the person, let me just say that Liberace was a gentleman and a class act when the spotlight was turned off and the curtain closed.

Liberace arrived at the course in a white, chauffeur-driven, stretch limousine, a vehicle that seemed to be a bumper or two longer than the putting green. Even though he was wearing sneakers, blue jeans and a white cotton pullover jersey, there could be no doubt, this was still Liberace – diamond rings glittered from his fingers, bracelets weighted down his wrists, golden chains hung around his neck. And the smile... well, who could ever forget his sincere, captivating smile. It was Liberace.

To tell you the truth, I'll never forget the sight of Liberace stepping out of the limo and walking toward me. There was just something about him, an aura, a wonderful, colorful aura. I could tell he genuinely cared about people and that's why people genuinely cared about him.

I continued to watch as he walked toward me. Twenty, maybe twenty five paces away, he waved and flashed that smile once again. There wasn't anything left to say except you had to like the man.

We went through a few minutes of formalities, just sort of getting to know each other. It was here that I called him Mr. Liberace, and he quickly corrected me. "Jim," he said, "all of my friends call me Lee."

Actually, our paths had crossed several times in the past, but this was our first real conversation, and Liberace soon pointed everything in the direction of golf. He was excited about his lesson. He was looking forward to the challenge.

Liberace told me that he really wanted to learn the game. "Working the way I do, nights and indoors, I need something of a hobby that will give me a little exercise and sunshine. Everyone tells me golf is exactly what I need."

With nothing left to say, Liberace asked his chauffeur to get his equipment so that we could get started. Now I really can't say for sure because I didn't actually use the stop watch, but I would venture a guess the chauffeur spent five, maybe ten minutes unloading enough golf equipment to stock a Nevada Bob's and then some.

In a tone that sounded apologetic, Liberace said, "I didn't know what I would need for my first lesson. So... I picked up a little bit of everything. I hope I didn't miss anything."

"Well, Lee" I said while taking a quick inventory of golf clubs and more golf clubs and every club imaginable, "we'll need one club for the lesson and I'll show you how to pack a bag – fourteen clubs per bag. I'll get you set up with the equipment you'll need. Then, you can return the rest of this and get your money back."

"Jim," Liberace looked into my eyes, and in a very sobering tone he spoke, "I don't care about money or the extra equipment. I care about one thing. I really want to learn how to golf. This is very important to me, Jim. I really want to learn how to hit the ball and play the game."

I had given a lot of lessons to a lot of different people in my time. But I had never seen anyone with a more serious expression than Liberace. He wanted to learn the game. "Don't worry," I answered, "you'll learn how to golf."

With that we were ready for the lesson to begin. But, there was a little problem. "Lee," I said, "it might be a little tough to grip and swing the club with all of your jewelry on."

Liberace apologized and began the ritual of removing the jewelry. He was putting everything in his chauffeur's hat – rings, bracelets, and even the gold chains.

"I almost feel naked when I take off all of my jewelry," he explained.

I could tell he was serious. The jewelry was a part of him. So, I told him that he didn't need to take off the gold chains, and that a bracelet or two wouldn't hurt. "In fact, if you want... You can keep the pinkie ring on the right hand. It won't hurt your grip."

"Are you sure? I don't want to do anything that will hurt my chances."

I smiled and replied, "Seriously, a bracelet, a few gold chains and the pinkie ring won't hurt your chances."

Liberace thanked me for letting him wear some jewelry during the lesson. And with that, Liberace put on his glove and we began.

I started with the limbering up and stretching out phase of the game. I went through a little bit of a routine and talked about muscle groups associated with the game of golf. Then I demonstrated the proper swing and told Liberace to try one.

Liberace took one practice swing, chunked the ground, and stung his hands a little bit. It wasn't anything serious, but suddenly he looked at me with a pale expression on his face. I thought he was going to pass out.

"My God..." he said. "I could have broken my hand or a finger."

I tried to tell him not to worry. Every golfer, at one time or another, hits a heavy shot. Golf courses are full of divots. In fact, most touring pros really go down after the ball.

It didn't matter what I said because Liberace was troubled. He was really upset. "Jim, I have a responsibility to my music and my fans. What would happen if I broke a finger and couldn't play?"

He dropped the club and stepped back from it as though it were a venomous snake. I didn't know what to say. It was obvious he was concerned about breaking a finger or hurting his hand. And to be honest, there was a remote possibility he could injure himself. But it was only a very remote possibility.

Several minutes later the color returned to his face and he asked, "Jim, could you do me a favor?"

"Well, of course. What is it?"

"Jim, please hit a golf ball for me. Hit a long one. Would you do that for me?"

I didn't quite understand but I pulled out my driver and teed up a ball. I took a couple of practice swings and then let one fly. Coming out of my shot a little the ball sort of ballooned up and faded. The drive was probably 250 yards, maybe a little more. It certainly wasn't my best effort.

I was going to tee up another ball, but I heard Liberace say, "Jim, that was absolutely wonderful."

He was still looking down range at the ball, his eyes sparkling with life, his face cracked in a full smile. "Simply astounding, Jim."

Then he turned, looked at me and said, "Thanks, Jim. Thanks for a wonderful day. I'll never forget this day." He laughed a little and continued, "My first golf lesson."

Taking off his glove, he put his jewelry back on. Then he pointed down range toward the ball I had just hit. "You'll never know how much I wish I could do that."

Once again he thanked me for the wonderful day, turned and began to walk away. I shouted to him, "You're forgetting your equipment."

He stopped and turned around. "You keep it." Holding out his hands and pretending to run his fingers over the keyboard, he said, "Golf is much too violent for me. You understand. And Jim, once again, you'll never know how much I wish I could do that. You know, hit a golf ball. Thanks for a really wonderful day."

I watched as he drove away and kept watching until the limo was completely gone. That, I told myself, was a brief encounter with a legend, a master entertainer, a very good man.

I found it truly amazing that he was impressed with the high fade I had hit. But more impressive was the fact that he actually made me feel important, very important.

Looking around I found myself standing knee deep in the finest collection of golf equipment money could buy. Anyone, I thought, can hit a golf ball, but there's only one Liberace.

Suddenly it slammed into me, that one moment of regret. As Liberace was making me feel important, I failed to tell him how special he was to me and how very special he was to all of his other fans throughout the world. I promised myself, the next time I saw him, I'd tell him how special he really was.

Several hours later, my phone rang. It was Liberace. He was playing at John Ascuaga's Nugget, and invited me to the show. He mentioned that he would leave two tickets for me and my wife.

I wanted to go to the show, but my mother was in town visiting. He had invited me and my wife and I didn't know if it was proper to bring my mother along. I started to bow out, but he quickly asked, "Do you need more than two passes, Jim?"

I started to explain that my mother was visiting, but before I could finish he interrupted. "Your mother... Jim, I think that's just wonderful... your mother has come for a visit. I'll leave three tickets. Is three enough?"

"Three will be perfect," I said.

We went to the show, sat in the front row, and Liberace introduced me as his golfing pro. He told me to stand up and made the audience give me a round of applause.

"I watched Jim hit a golf ball today... it must have traveled three hundred yards. Gee..." Liberace looked directly at me, "You'll never know how much I wish I could do that, Jim. But I might hurt my fingers. And my fingers are the reason I can afford to buy these kind of things." He flashed his rings, pointed to his costume and the audience laughed.

And once again, I felt important. Liberace made me feel important.

Then he introduced my mother and my wife. He made them stand up and told the audience to give them a round of applause. He said wonderful things about wives and mothers and women in general. He made my mother and my wife feel important... We all deserve to feel important once in a while.

After the show he invited us backstage. I wanted to thank him for the tickets, and for making me feel important. But I didn't get a chance. Instead, Liberace thanked me for coming to the show and taking time to come backstage. He made us feel as though we were doing him a big favor by spending time with him.

Then he began to show my wife and mother some of his jewelry and costumes. Before long they were trying on some of his jewelry as he gave them the history of each piece. He spent an hour with us... an hour of quality time. Then someone said he had to get ready for the next show.

Liberace again thanked me for coming, hugged my mother and wife, and was gone. A moment later, I realized I had failed to thank him for making us feel important. Once again I told myself, the next time I see him, I'll let him know just how special he really is.

Unfortunately, I never saw Liberace again. There are times when I think about him and his first and only golf lesson. Really, I should have told him anyone can hit a golf ball. But it took a special person to lift the weight of the world off weary shoulders with a smile and music.

For some reason, I think Liberace knew the truth about the little things I could do for a few people, and the great things he was chosen to do for many. Yes, Liberace had to know he was special. And in being special he made others feel important simply because he was first and foremost humble. Anyone can hit a golf ball, but there was only one Liberace.

And God bless Liberace.

Lieutenant Columbo

I was teaching at the Studio City Golf Course in Los Angeles when comedian Buddy Lester introduced me to Peter Falk. Peter was an avid golfer and a very good stick, but like all amateurs, his game needed a little tweaking. I gave him a lesson and the next thing I knew he was inviting Buddy and me to play a round of golf at Brentwood Country Club.

Brentwood Country Club, for those of you who don't golf the Los Angeles circuit, is very exclusive and posh. In addition, Brentwood is an excellent golf course. I looked at Buddy and Buddy looked at me. We quickly accepted the invitation even though we weren't sure Peter was a member of Brentwood. It didn't matter who the member was. Buddy and I were invited to Brentwood and we were going.

However, since I had been working all morning, I wanted to clean up a little and change clothes. "I'm a little scuffed up," I told Peter. "So, give me a few minutes to change clothes and I'll be ready."

But Peter looked me up and down and said, "You're fine. Get your clubs and let's go. I'll drive."

I did as instructed and went to get my clubs. Still, I couldn't help but think I should get cleaned up a little. Once again, I mentioned a change of clothes to Peter. And once again he said it wasn't necessary. "Trust me. You're fine. We don't want to be over dressed."

Judging from Peter's last statement, I got the impression he wasn't changing clothes either. If I thought I looked a little scuffed up, then Peter looked as though he had been sleeping in his clothes for a week or so. His clothes were, shall I say, a little wrinkled and then some.

Suddenly clothes were no longer an issue because we had arrived at Peter's car. He drove a black, very small Mercedes... I think.

Now if I thought I looked a little scuffed and that Peter looked as though he had been sleeping in his clothes, then his car resembled something that had been through World Wars I & II. I'm serious. Peter's car must have been bombed, torpedoed and used as a target at the artillery range. It was a wreck.

Peter started jamming our clubs in his little trunk. And how he managed to get three sets of clubs to fit in that small area, I'll never know. Fortunately, my set of clubs went in second. Buddy Lester wasn't so lucky. His clubs went in the trunk last. It took a little bending, pushing and forcing, but Peter managed to get Buddy's clubs in the trunk, too. I was glad those were Buddy's sticks and not mine.

Then came the best part of all. Peter told us, "Get in. Let's go."

Buddy and I tried to get in. However, the interior was cluttered with papers, cigar butts, soda bottles and an assortment of debris that made entering difficult. Buddy and I were trying to be diplomatic. We were sort of skirting around the debris when Peter suddenly started brushing everything off the seats and onto the floor. "Come on," he said, "we don't have all day. Get in."

As we rode toward Brentwood, I honestly thought Peter would go into the locker room and take the wrinkles off his clothes. You know, sort of straighten up a little because this was, of course, Brentwood. But upon arrival at the club, Peter parked the auto, got out and went around to the trunk. It soon became obvious. He wasn't going to change clothes in the locker room. I guess he wasn't a member after all.

With our clubs on the ground, Peter started rummaging around the trunk. He mumbled something about shoes. Then, under an old paper bag, low and behold, he found one shoe. The second shoe was tucked behind some other debris.

He dropped the shoes on the ground and continued searching the trunk for something else. Mumbling to himself, I heard him say, "I know I put a pair in here, but where are they?"

A moment later, Peter found what he had been looking for, a pair of socks. At least I thought it was a pair of socks.

Here we were, in the middle of the parking lot at Brentwood Country Club and Peter was changing socks and shoes. He sat down on the bumper and took off his shoes and socks. Then he grabbed one of the "athletic socks" and attempted to put it on.

The sock was a little stiff. Crusty would be another word that could describe it. But nonetheless, Peter was determined to force his foot into the sock. And suddenly, just as I suspected, I heard the rip and saw Peter's foot go through the sock.

Buddy and I wanted to laugh, but not in Peter's face. So, we sort of covered our mouths and snickered a little. But at the same time we were watching Peter. And to our surprise, he went about his business as though nothing had happened. He tucked the torn end of the sock under his toe and put on the shoe.

We played our round of golf and it was an enjoyable round at that. As a matter of fact, I always enjoyed playing with Peter. He was a good stick and a terrific person. But my first encounter with him always stuck in my mind because on that particular day he was such a marvelous, wonderful character – wrinkled, scuffed up and yet he got from point A to point B with a degree of precision.

Then one day I was watching a television show called Columbo. And there he was, on television, Peter Falk as Lieutenant Columbo. Suddenly it hit me. I didn't golf with Peter Falk. Instead, I went to Brentwood with Inspector Columbo.

Dirty Harry

My stories about Hollywood usually fall into two categories. I have stories that will make people laugh and I have stories that will touch people. But my association with Clint Eastwood is neither a belly laugh nor a revelation. My story about Clint Eastwood falls in the category of regret, a regret on my part. Let me explain.

I was not only Director of Golf at the Elkhorn Lodge & Golf Club in Sun Valley, Idaho, but I was also running the Jim Chenoweth School of Golf. With Clint having a big home up in the mountains and his love for the game of golf, it seemed natural that he and I would eventually bump into each other on some fairway at the course. But our perchance meeting never happened over a round of golf. It actually took place at the lodge.

I had heard that Clint and his production company were in town to shoot the movie *Pale Rider*. And as it was, one night after work, I stopped by the lodge for a drink and a bite to eat. I placed my order and happened to glance at the table next to mine. There were six or seven guys sitting at the table, but one person really looked familiar. Suddenly it hit me – Clint Eastwood.

I introduced myself and mentioned that I was the Director of Golf.

With the magic word golf, Clint told me to join him and his crew for a drink and dinner.

It turned out to be an enjoyable evening. We talked about movie making and golf. Both subjects were favorite of mine and Clint's. As the evening wore on, I invited Clint and his crew to play golf any time they wanted, and Clint invited me to the set of *Pale Rider*.

The next day I took Clint up on his offer. I found it fascinating, watching how a movie was made. But even more fascinating was Clint's eye for detail. He was not only a great actor, but an incredible director. He was a perfectionist, an absolute perfectionist. Everything had to be in place and it was the same with everyone working behind the camera or standing in front of it.

Several days later, after finishing my work at the school, I decided to get a few holes of golf in before dark. At the pro shop, one of my assistants

Me; Clint Eastwood; Dave Pfannenstein, my assistant; and Clint's stand-in and friend, on the set of "Pale Rider."

pointed toward the first tee and asked, "Do you know who that is?"

Of course, it was Clint. He had taken me up on my offer and had just teed off with another of my assistants, David Pfannenstein. I caught up to Clint and David just as they were ready to hit their second shots.

The first hole was a long par five and Clint, along with David, laid up. But being an adventuresome soul, I dropped a ball, pulled out a three wood and took a pretty good swing. The ball landed on the green and rolled to within fifteen feet of the flag.

Clint remarked, "Great shot." And with that he began asking questions about the swing. We played a few holes and during that time I gave Clint some tips. His approach to the game of golf was no different from the way he worked on his movies. Clint Eastwood was a perfectionist, a man who always wanted to do his absolute best.

During the filming of *Pale Rider*, I spent a lot of time on the set watching Clint work and he spent some time with me learning the finer points of the game of golf. Clint was a very good athlete and I always believed he could have mastered the game of golf. But his one problem was time. He was always so busy working that he just didn't have much time for golf or lessons.

Suddenly *Pale Rider* was completed and Clint was gone. But then, three or four months later, I ran into him at the Crosby up in Pebble Beach. Clint was at the driving range getting warmed up before teeing off for the Pro-Am. We talked for a few minutes and the next thing I knew, I was giving Clint a lesson.

The next year, at the Crosby, I ran into Clint again. And, just like the previous year, we talked a little and a few minutes later, I was giving him a lesson. Clint had a passion for the game and had potential, and with his athletic talent, he could have become an excellent player. Even to this day, I have always believed that if a teaching pro would have spent some time with Clint, he would have become one of the best golfers in the entertainment industry.

As a teaching pro, I take a certain pleasure in being able to help individuals find a better game. And I guess that's why my story about Clint Eastwood becomes one of regret. To this day, I regret that I didn't make an extra effort to spend time with Clint. After all, I had his phone number at Warner Brothers and was often in Los Angeles. It wouldn't have taken much on my part to pick up the phone and give Clint a call. Sure, Clint probably would have been busy. Still, we could have stopped by a driving range and hit a bucket of balls or perhaps even found time to play a few holes. But I never called, and the only times I saw Clint would be at the Crosby. And every year it was always the same. We would engage in a little bit of a conversation and then it would end up as a quick lesson. It was obvious Clint wanted a better game, but as a teaching pro, I certainly missed one there.

###

My assistant, Dave; the home run king, Roger Maris and me, the king of the links, Jim Chenoweth.

Frankie "Beach Blanket" Avalon, one of the better players I've worked with. I really enjoyed him. He was a real gentleman.

Willie Mays; Jim Chenoweth; Billy Wilson, former San Francisco 49er; and Claude Crabbe, former Los Angeles Ram.

Ron Gaylord and Burt Holiday. If you haven't heard of these guys, that's because, believe it or not, they were born before me.

Close friend and #1 assistant, Dave Pfannenstein.

6

Caddies,
A Dying Breed

To write a book about my adventures *From Tee To Green To Hollywood* and not tell a few caddie stories would almost be sacrileges. In this, the modern era of golf, it seems caddies are a vanishing breed. Oh sure, we see caddies out on tour with our favorite PGA pros, and there are a few golf purists at local clubs who still insist on walking eighteen with a caddie packing their bag. But for the most part, golf carts carry our clubs and we figure out the yardage to the flag without the assistance of a Caddie. Still, I remember a day when caddies were as much a part of the game as our favorite club. And with that, let me tell you just a few of my favorite caddie stories.

Can I Get Home From Here?

Bing Crosby was not known as a long ball hitter. In fact, I would categorize Bing as less than average off the tee but extremely accurate. He rarely missed a fairway with the driver. But one day, Bing careened a tee shot and that was the first time I ever heard him utter those six words, "Can I get home from here?"

As the story goes, Bing and I were playing the Scottsdale Country Club in Scottsdale, Arizona. Since it was a warm, but comfortable day, Bing suggested that we get a couple of caddies and walk. A little exercise sounded like a good idea to me.

On a par five, Bing really got ahold of a tee shot. He hit one dead solid perfect with a little bit of a draw and a whole lot of roll. I had played a lot of golf with Bing and this was probably his career long drive. It was such a long drive that Bing was in unfamiliar territory. He stood beside his ball for nearly a minute looking toward the green... a well-bunkered green with problems left and right. To get home in two, he would have to hit one about 200 yards.

It always took Bing at least three shots to reach the greens on par fives. But today was different. I could tell he was thinking about trying to get home in two.

Since we were having a little match, I didn't think he was going to ask me what I thought. Of course he could get home in two. It's like I said, Bing was very accurate and a good three wood would put him on the green putting for an eagle. But just in case he did ask my advice, I was ready to caution him about the little cross breeze and suggest that he "play safe and lay up."

As I thought, Bing never asked my advice. He threw a few blades of grass into the air and saw the breeze gently blowing left to right. Finally, he turned to his Caddie, Jeff Thomsen, and asked, "Jeff, can I get home from here?"

Jeff looked at Bing with a perplexed expression on his face. And, in a very apologetic way he answered, "Gee, Mr. Crosby, I'm sorry, but I can't answer that question. I don't know where you live."

Eventually Bing composed himself long enough to take a swing at the ball. And I am happy to report that we tied the hole. Bing and I two-putted for birdies.

###

Pebble Beach
& Old Willie

I was playing in the Crosby for the first time, and naturally, I wanted to make a good impression. After all, as a competitor, I had my pride. And also, Bing and I were pretty good friends by now. I guess I wanted to show Bing that I could compete with the big boys.

Arriving at Pebble Beach early on a misty and cold Monday morning, I was looking forward to a couple of good days of practice before the tournament started. This would not only be my first experience playing in the Crosby, but it would be the first time I played Pebble Beach. I wanted to get familiar with the layout, especially if we would have to play the course under these conditions – foggy, misty and cold.

With my caddie running late, I carried my bag to the practice range and started hitting balls. A few minutes later, I bumped into Bob Duden, a pro from the Portland area. Bob had an opening in his group and suggested that I join him. "We're teeing off in about fifteen minutes," Bob said.

I wanted to play with Bob because he was a good stick and I enjoyed his company. But I had to tell him, "My caddie is late or lost."

"Hey, wait a second, here," Bob said. "Remember that colored guy who packed your bag up in Portland?"

"Old Willie?" I asked.

"Yeah, Old Willie. I saw him sleeping under a tree over there." Bob pointed toward a grouping of Oaks. "Maybe he can pack your bag today."

Walking toward the trees, I saw Old Willie snoozing, just like Bob said. It was cold, misty and foggy, and yet Old Willie was sleeping like a baby.

"Hey, Willie! Wake up!"

Old Willie opened his eyes, looked up and said, "Mr. Chenoweth. I didn't know you were playin' in the Crosby."

We had several moments of idle conversation and then I asked Old Willie if he was packing anyone's bag. He informed me that he had been following the tour, picking up work wherever and whenever he could, but as yet, he hadn't landed a job.

"Perfect," I said. "You need a job and I need a caddie. I've never played Pebble before so I can use an experienced guy like you."

Old Willie was about to say something, but I interrupted. We were running a little late so I told Old Willie where my bag was and that I would meet him on the first tee.

I hit a good drive on the first hole, but with the air being cold and heavy, I felt it was still a four, maybe five iron to the green. It just looked like a long way to the green.

"Oh, no, Mr. Chenoweth," Old Willie spoke up as I asked for the five iron. "I remember, you're long with the irons. It's no more than a good eight, maybe nine iron for you."

The shot looked longer than an eight iron, but Old Willie insisted it was only 150 yards to the green. I guess it was the fog, the mist, and my unfamiliarity with the course that made me think it was more than a good eight iron.

Taking my caddie's advice, I hit the eight iron, and a second later I heard Old Willie say, "No, no... you didn't get all of that one, Mr. Chenoweth."

Old Willie was right. I didn't get all of that eight iron, but I did hit it reasonably well. When I got to the ball, I was surprised to see it was still forty yards short of the green.

Chipping up, I missed my putt for par. And, as we walked off the green, I told Old Willie I thought it was more than an eight iron. But Old Willie insisted it was nothing more than a "good" eight iron. "You jus' didn't hit it good, Mr. Chenoweth."

Maybe Old Willie was right. Maybe I didn't get as much of that eight iron as I thought. And the other thing I had to consider was the fact I never walked the course before. At least Willie wasn't seeing Pebble for the first time.

After several more holes and several more times of listening to Old Willie's advice, I saw a degree of consistency in my game. I was either two clubs long or three clubs short. In other words, I wasn't hitting many greens in regulation.

Suddenly I remembered what happened the last time Old Willie packed my bag. It wasn't that Old Willie did a bad job in Portland. It was just that several weeks after the tournament I found Old Willie had left something of his in my bag – a bottle of MD 20/20.

Being a classy guy, I wasn't suggesting that Old Willie was drinking on the job. But considering the fact he had walked Pebble before, his yardage and club selection was leaving a lot to be desired. So, instead of coming right out and accusing Old Willie of being drunk, I moved in for the sniff test. Whoa... now that was a mistake.

Other than the fact I immediately came to the conclusion Old Willie wasn't practicing oral hygiene on a regular basis, I could not detect the odor of wine, whiskey or any other adult beverage. He wasn't drunk and he was wearing glasses. So, it had to be the fog and mist. Poor visibility was throwing Old Willie off a little on his yardage and club selection.

On the back nine the sun broke through and I finally saw Pebble Beach in all of its natural beauty. With a break in the weather, I naturally figured that Old Willie would show a little improvement in clubbing me.

Old Willie called it a perfect drive and I had to agree. Standing in the middle of the fairway, I was thinking a wedge, but Old Willie said, "Eight iron, Mr. Chenoweth."

"Eight iron?" I asked. "We're only 120 yards out."

"Yeah, Mr. Chenoweth, but it's up hill, the pin is back and the hole plays a lot longer. Trust me. It's a smooth eight iron."

Call me foolish, but I backed off the thought of hitting a wedge and asked Old Willie for a nine iron. Old Willie reluctantly handed me the nine iron while saying "You gonna have to really hit the nine iron to get there... I mean really hit it good."

I still had a hard time believing it was a nine iron to the flag. But Old Willie did say the hole was playing up hill and the pin was in the back. He probably had seen this shot a hundred times before. So, I made it a good nine iron, a real good nine iron.

"Oh, my, Mr. Chenoweth," Old Willie said. "I didn't mean for you to hit that good of a nine iron."

Now had this particular hole been twenty-five yards longer, or my drive twenty five yards shorter, my real good nine iron would have no doubt covered the flag. But since it was only an easy wedge in and not a real good nine iron, Old Willie and I were looking for my ball where professional golfers are not supposed to hit balls. Double bogey! I could only wonder what would have happened had I not hit the perfect drive.

After that I stopped asking Old Willie questions about yardage and club selection. I simply guessed my way back toward the club house and ended up with a hard-fought 75. I paid Old Willie and thanked him. But then he asked if I was going back toward town. He needed a ride.

I found my wife Betty in the clubhouse and the three of us took off. Driving down the coast it was a magnificent sight – the terrain, the ocean, the sun breaking through the clouds. Finally Old Willie broke the silence. "I can hardly wait to tell my family that I finally got to see Pebble Beach."

I looked in the mirror at Old Willie sitting in the back seat and asked, "Finally got to see Pebble Beach? You make it sound as though you've never seen Pebble before today."

"That's what I was trying to tell you when we got started. Remember, Mr. Chenoweth? Remember when you interrupted me and said to hurry up and get your bag 'cause we was running late."

The next day I had my regular caddie. But unlike my experience with Old Willie, I never asked my caddie for yardage or advice. I just told myself, let's see, yesterday I was over there and Old Willie said to hit the eight iron. So... that meant I could hit a hard three iron or maybe an easy wedge. Either way it didn't matter because I was playing Pebble and Pebble was a little taste of paradise.

The Gunner & A Caddie Called Lil' Abner

Honestly, I can't remember exactly where I met The Gunner or when. His real name was Bob Prince and he was the radio voice of the Pittsburgh Pirates. I think I met The Gunner when I was the Director of Golf at the Sahara.

The Gunner was the type of guy a person could meet for the first time and swear they had known him all of their life. Make no mistake about it, The Gunner was a Prince in more ways than just name alone.

At any rate, when The Gunner called and asked me to play in his Pro-Am in the Pittsburgh area, I said yes without any hesitation. The Gunner's tournament was a two-day affair with the profits going to charity. One round of golf was played at Williams Country Club outside of Wheeling, West Virginia, and the other round was played at Virginia

Country Club near Pittsburgh. If it sounds confusing, it really wasn't.

Arriving at Williams Country Club, I could tell from the very beginning it was going to be a first class affair. There were former professional basketball players there – Jerry West and John Havlicek just to name a few, as well as a host of Pittsburgh Steelers and Cleveland Browns. And The Gunner couldn't have picked a better place to play. Williams Country Club was an absolutely beautiful golf course in the mountains of West Virginia.

When I caught up with The Gunner, he started apologizing. It had to do with the caddie who was going to pack my bag. The Gunner said, "Jim, the caddie assigned to your bag isn't a pro. And worst of all, he's a little slow... not the brightest person I've ever met. I'm sorry, but I just found out what had happened and it's too late to make a change."

I understood what The Gunner was talking about. Since there was a purse for the professional golfers, The Gunner thought I would be at a real disadvantage. Not only would I be on a strange golf course, but I wouldn't have a pro packing my bag.

I told Gunner my Pebble Beach and Old Willie story. And then I let him know I didn't come for the purse. I came because he asked me to come. I was there because of Bob Prince, his charity, and nothing else really mattered. I was here to have some fun and help out The Gunner.

Then, I met my caddie. He was a little guy who, from one angle looked eighteen years old, and from another angle, I'd swear he was sixty. I couldn't get a handle on his age. I've never seen anyone who looked young and old. Do you know what I mean? The caddie sort of reminded me of that guy on the cover of MAD Magazine, Alfred E. Newman. Where was Old Willie when I needed him?

"I ain't never toted a sack like this before," he told me with a big grin.

Well, I thought it was a grin. I really couldn't be certain because most of his front teeth were missing.

Actually, when he picked up my bag by the handle and started dragging it like a big, ol' clumsy suitcase, I quickly came to the conclusion he ain't never toted a sack like that before.

"Hold it! Hold it!" I said. "Now let me show you something."

I pointed to the shoulder strap and asked, "Now what do you think this is for?"

"I don't know," he answered. "It's like I done tol' you. I ain't never toted a sack like this before."

I took the shoulder strap, put it over his shoulder and said, "There. Carry it that way. And, it's not a sack. It's called a bag."

"All be darn... " He said. "That's slick... Really slick. I ain't never seen a bag like this before."

The tournament started and the boy was having trouble keeping up with me. In truth it was actually the refreshment cart that created the problem. When the refreshment cart came along, and it seemed like every minute or so, he would put the bag down and have a drink. Then he couldn't figure out how to get the strap back up over his shoulder.

Finally, I took five minutes and taught him how to use the shoulder strap. In the long run, I figured it would save a lot of time. You know... instead of me helping him get the strap over his shoulder every time he set the bag down, I'd invest a little time and teach him how to do it. At first it was a little confusing, but he finally caught on. And boy was he proud of himself.

Three, maybe four holes into the tournament, the boy started complaining about my heavy bag. Then he started complaining about the heat. It was hot... and humid. Then he had another drink. I think he was consuming adult beverages – beer, a lot of beer and he was getting a little surly.

It might have been the fifth hole when I took out my driver and sent the boy up ahead to give the all clear signal. The hole played uphill and was a dog leg left. Since we couldn't see the group in front of us, we wanted to make sure they were gone before we teed off.

Well, he gave the all clear signal and we hit. And several minutes later, Ray Mansfield, the center for the Pittsburgh Steelers was standing on the crown of the hill screaming back at us. We had hit into Ray's group. In fact, my tee shot nearly hit him in the head. For the record, Ray weighed in around 290 pounds and was a little more than slightly upset.

I walked up the fairway and apologized to Ray explaining we had sent the caddie up ahead for the all clear signal. Ray glared at the caddie and asked in a grumpy way, "Didn't you see us?"

"Sure enough did see ya'. Heck, ya'll were standin' right out in the open. Couldn't miss ya'."

"Then why the hell did you tell them to hit?" Ray beat me to the obvious question. My caddie pointed toward the green and said, "I thought they wanted me to tell 'em when those folks stood up the little flag and walked away from the smooth grass."

Ray looked at the caddie for several moments and then turn toward me. He just shook his head back and forth. "Hey..." Ray stammered a little. "I'm sorry about my temper. I didn't understand what kind of an uphill battle you were facing."

Ray got back in his golf cart and drove up the fairway to join his group on the smooth grass.

Naturally, we waited for Ray and his group to putt out and get far away from the green. That way we wouldn't have any more problems. But that's when I realized I had a little problem of my own.

When I sent my caddie up ahead to give us the all-clear signal, he didn't realize that meant taking the bag with him. And now, here I stood, in the middle of the fairway without golf clubs. My clubs were missing.

"Do you realize my clubs are missing?" I was, for the time being, speaking in a polite manner.

The caddie looked at me for a moment and then asked, "So... what do you want me to do about it?"

"Well I expect you to go back and get my clubs."

"But I don't remember where I left 'em," the caddie said with a little anger evident in his voice.

Imagine that, my caddie was getting POed with me because he had forgotten my clubs. Realizing the boy probably had a little too much to drink, I nonetheless still had to put my foot down. I had to let the boy have a piece of my mind. So, I explained who the caddie was and who was playing golf. Then I said, "It's your responsibility to tote the bag, sack, suitcase or whatever you want to call it, and I'll worry about hitting the ball up to the smooth grass."

"At's stupid," he said. "How's come I have to carry the big bag while all them little bitty bags are packed on them funny little cars? Huh? How's come me and you have to walk and everybody else gets to ride on them funny little cars? Huh?"

The question sort of surprised me a little and I didn't have an answer on the tip of my tongue. Most of the Pro-Ams have a policy whereby the amateurs and celebrities ride in golf carts while the pros walk. I could have explained that I was a professional and they were amateurs. In other words, I made my living as a professional golfer and the amateurs were out just for fun. But the boy wouldn't understand that logic. In fact, I wasn't even sure I understood that logic.

Then, I thought, wait a second here... why do all them people with the little bitty bags ride in them funny lookin' cars while a guy like me has to walk? And furthermore, not only do I have to walk, but I have to hire a caddie to tote my sack?

The caddie was still waiting for my answer when The Gunner pulled up in a cart with my bag. "Jim," he said. "Did you lose something?"

"I didn't but someone did," I answered while looking at my caddie.

The Gunner put my clubs on one of the amateur's carts and told the caddie that he was going to take him for a ride... a ride which I was positive would end at the front gate to Williams Country Club.

I finished the tournament with my clubs riding and me walking. And actually, after The Gunner took the caddie for that ride, everything was uneventful. Well... except for the dinner afterwards. I just had to ask The Gunner that lingering question, the question I couldn't answer when the caddie originally asked it. So, when I saw Bob Prince at dinner I asked, "Gunner, how come all the people with the little bitty bags get to ride them funny little cars while guys like me have to tote our heavy bags?"

The Gunner looked at me with a wry grin and his best radio voice said, "Jimmy, I'm going to give you the same answer I gave your caddie when he asked that very question. Because, just because, that's why they ride and you walk."

The Bob Hope Desert Classic

I'm not sure my first (and last) experience at The Bob Hope Desert Classic qualifies as a caddie story. However, rather than blame the entire incident on nerves, I would have to say that part of my misadventures could be attributed to a caddie who deserted me when things got a little sticky. For what it is worth, here is an account of my trip to the desert.

Receiving my first invitation to play in the Hope, I was naturally quite excited. After all, it was a big tournament, a tournament which attracted the best touring pros in the world and the greatest names in Hollywood.

Of course I wouldn't be one of the favorites to win the tournament, but I viewed my trip to Palm Springs as positive sign in two categories. First of all my career as a professional golfer had to be gaining some recognition or else I wouldn't have been invited. And secondly, from a position of strictly business, I would be hobnobbing with movie stars and all types of celebrities. Sure my client list of Hollywood's golfing aficionados was growing, but I was always looking for new business. After all, I had a wife and children. And, over the years, my family had developed some bad habits such as expecting a roof over their heads and wanting to see food on the table during dinner time.

Some of my original excitement about the tournament waned when I told my caddie, Elroy, about our invitation. For some reason, Elroy didn't show much emotion.

I asked, "Elroy, what's wrong?"

When Elroy quietly explained that some of the country clubs in Palm Springs didn't permit colored caddies on the course, the wind was knocked out of my sails. Elroy was, as I said, my caddie. But in some areas of Palm Springs, Elroy would be considered a colored caddie instead of a tremendous human being.

In my excitement I had forgotten that although we lived in a free country, not all of us were free. Well... if Elroy couldn't go, I'd pass on the tournament.

But Elroy stepped in and explained the facts – a family, a roof over everyone's head, and food on the table. Okay... I'd go to the tournament, but I wanted Elroy to know he would still be paid his share of my purse. I promised Elroy I'd give it my best effort.

Finally, the day came and I was there, at the Bob Hope Desert Classic. It was only the practice round but I was nervous and uptight. After all, this was, as I've already mentioned, my first invitation to the Hope! The best pros in the world were here along with some of the worst golfers in the entertainment industry. With the pros playing for a lot of prize money and the entertainers simply hacking up the course, I didn't want any misconceptions as to why I had been invited. But with my desire to play my best and earn a paycheck for my family and Elroy, I put a lot of pressure on myself.

I was aware of the fact that if a person came to the golf course nervous and uptight, they were in for a bad day. As a matter of fact, I think every golfer knows that once a person gets nervous and uptight, anything can happen and all of it is going to be bad. And yet, I managed to take a little case of nerves and being uptight into a record-setting bad day on the course. In fact, my experience during the Bob Hope Desert Classic makes Greg Norman's 1996 Sunday collapse at the Masters look like a triumphant victory march of a conquering Caesar coming home to Rome.

Arriving at the course, I met my caddie. After about ten seconds of conversation, I was really missing Elroy.

To begin with, my caddie was upset. He mumbled something about drawing an "entertainer" instead of a professional golfer.

"But hey," I told the caddie. "Cheer up. I am not an entertainer. I'm a pro. Jim Chenoweth from Reno."

"Entertainer or hack pro, it's the same thing," the Caddie said. "The tournament doesn't start until the weekend. I wanted to draw a pro who would still be here on Sunday and not some guy sitting in his living room back in Reno."

For those of you who don't understand the impact of that particular statement, let me explain. The caddie was telling me that I wouldn't make the cut. In other words, the checks are passed out on Sunday and to get a check a pro has to play on Sunday.

If my introduction to the caddie didn't tell me I was in for a bad day, then my first couple of swings at the driving range screamed the message loud and clear. I couldn't find any rhythm with my swing. It was slice, hook, chunk, twang – my God, I shanked one.

The caddie sort of rolled his eyes back and quietly repeated my words, "I'm a pro. Jim Chenoweth from Reno."

I was going to say something to the caddie, but then, I overheard several people in the gallery talking about me. I listened in hoping they were going to say something nice.

Well, they didn't say anything nice and yet it wasn't all that bad. They were looking at a program and trying to figure out what movie they had seen me in. Didn't anyone around here understand I wasn't an entertainer? I was a pro and yet I was getting no respect.

Suddenly it dawned on me. Now I knew why they didn't invited Rodney Dangerfield to the tournament. They had Jim Chenoweth.

Ten, maybe fifteen minutes later, as I walked from the range to the first tee, a little old lady stepped out of the crowd and said, "You're my favorite person of all times. May I have your autograph?"

"And just who do you think I am?" I asked in a polite manner.

To be perfectly honest, I was hoping she would say, Jim Chenoweth, or any golfer for that matter.

"Oh, come on now," she said with a smile. "I'd know you anywhere. You're Robert Mitchum."

I figured what the heck and signed the autograph, "Best Wishes, Bob Mitchum." At least someone would be able to look back on this day and smile.

Further complicating everything and adding to my nervousness was Arnold Palmer. Arnold was playing in the group in front of me. Now a person has to understand that when Arnold Palmer played, his legions lined the fairways in unbelievable numbers. And today, Arnie's Army was out in such force that they were lined up five and six rows deep from tee to green. Sure they were there to watch Arnie, but the stragglers would still get a look at the pro following on the heels of the King.

We teed off and after several holes I was beginning to think my life might be better served if I could get into the movie business. Gee, if that old gal had me confused with Mitchum, maybe I could bluff my way into a motion picture or two. At least if I made a bad movie I could hide out in my Beverly Hills mansion. But out here, on the golf course, there wasn't any place to hide. And believe me. I was looking.

I was really struggling and the pressure was mounting. Of course, right up in front of me, Mr. Palmer was playing his typical game of Smart Bomb accuracy. But the SCUD Missiles were being launched by the guy in the next group – yours truly.

In the worst way, I wanted to survive the cut and get a check on Sunday for my wife, my kids and Elroy. I wanted to be here on Sunday just to shove everything down my caddie's throat. But things were not going well.

Nerves, pressure, whatever the reason, I was hitting golf balls all over the place. Before long members of Arnie's Army were falling back and watching me. What the heck, they all knew Arnie was making nothing but pars and birdies. Boring stuff. But that guy behind Arnie was a different story. He was some kind of a comedian or something. A really funny guy.

"He must be one of them Vegas comedians," I heard someone in the crowd say. "You know, one of them guys who warms up the audience for the star."

Wow! I had just been reduced from Robert Mitchum, silver screen legend, to the warm-up act for a Las Vegas show. Talk about pressure. And then my caddie wasn't helping either. He kept reminding me that I would be in Reno on Sunday and he would be jobless. I liked it better when they thought I was Robert Mitchum.

Now, I really had to show the gallery I wasn't in the entertainment business. I was a golfer. A professional golfer. I earned my living doing this kind of stuff... Well, not exactly this kind of stuff, but I did earn my living by playing golf.

Any thoughts of convincing the crowd I was a golfer and not a hacker from the entertainment community, probably went out the window when I snap hooked my next tee shot. With a disgusted expression on his face, my caddie said something about "water."

"Water?" I asked while looking at the caddie in a semi-quizzical way. This was Palm Springs. Sure it was a desert, and I knew there were water hazards all over the place. But I just wasn't quite sure there was water along the left side of this particular fairway. I simply looked at the Caddie and sort of asked, "Water?"

The caddie stood there for a second or two looking at me as though I had asked the all-time dumbest question in the history of man. Finally, in a condescending way, he said, "Yes, water. You know, water as in wet! The stuff we drink. The stuff we take a bath in."

Then the caddie turned and started up the fairway. But after several steps he looked back at me and said, "Maybe you haven't figured it out just yet, but there is a reason they call this course Indian Wells, and there's a very good reason why the checks are passed out on Sunday."

The pressure had made a wreck out of me. I was thinking negative thoughts and hitting bad shots. My mind simply wasn't working. I'd try to concentrate but I couldn't. I was miserable. Suddenly golf wasn't much fun. And then my caddie, my own caddie was sticking a knife in my back every chance he had. Things couldn't get any worse. Or could they?

Unfortunately, I was only minutes away from discovering the answer to my last question. Not only could things get worse, but they would. Little did I know but thus far my day had actually taken place on the high ground. Now things were going to start downhill.

Of course the caddie was right, and he let me know it. "See. That's water. And that's your ball in the water... exactly where I said you hit it."

Okay, the ball was in the water, but playable. I caught a break. The ball had come to rest at the edge of the water and was sort of setting up. I could take a one stroke penalty and drop on dry land, or I could play the ball out of the water with no penalty stroke. Playing the ball meant my right foot would be in the water, my left on dry land, but the green would be reachable if I could hit a good shot.

Maybe, I told myself, if I hit a good shot I could turn things around. Maybe, I could put the pressure and negativism to rest and finish strongly. Maybe a good shot would even be enough to shut my caddie up. He was getting on my nerves.

My caddie was staring at me and when we made eye contact he said, "Look, you're having trouble hitting the ball when you're standing on dry land and it's teed up. So don't be stupid. Take a stroke and drop."

Stupid, I thought. My caddie was calling me stupid!

Right about now I wanted to take out my driver and hit something other than a golf ball. My caddie was turning vicious. But wait a second here. There was a reason he was the caddie packing my bag and a reason I was the pro swinging the club. I decided to go for it, to show the caddie who was boss. And perhaps this way I could even muzzle the wise guy in the crowd who thought I was a Vegas warm-up act. Yeah, I told myself, maybe this way I could show the crowd I was a professional golfer and not a hack actor.

I checked out the yardage to the flag and grabbed a club. But my caddie was shooting off his mouth again. "I know what you're thinking," my caddie said. "Playing bad is one thing but don't compound it by playing stupid. Take a stroke and drop."

I glared at my caddie for several cold moments. Then I sat down on the ground and started taking off my shoe and sock. I was nervous, uptight and POed!

Rolling up my pant leg I heard the crowd murmurer as someone said, "I don't believe this guy. Look at what he's doing."

Great I thought. Everyone is really getting into it. They're all behind me. They're all waiting for me to hit a good shot.

My caddie mumbled something, but I quickly retorted, "Not now, I'm concentrating." I had to assert myself, to let the caddie know he was working for me. I glared at him for a second or two as he shook his head back and forth. Finally he shrugged his shoulders and said, "Fine, do it your way... but... you'll be sorry."

I dismissed the caddie's remark by telling myself, "no guts, no glory."

Of course I hadn't practiced the shot, but I felt I could pull it off. I placed one foot on dry land, the other foot in the water and steadied myself. It was important to remain steady throughout the shot.

I took a good swing as a few drops of water sprayed up and hit me in the face, but the ball was gone. Looking toward the green, I remember whispering the word, "Amazing."

And it was amazing. I had pulled the shot off and a great shot it was. The ball hit on the front of the green and rolled to within five feet. I looked at the caddie and let my expression say it all. He understood. He could carry the bag and I'd hit the shots.

But something strange was going on here. Instead of cheers and applause, the crowd was falling down laughing. I simply didn't understand. What the heck was going on?

I sat down in order to put my sock and shoe back on. But now, the chorus of laughter, and I do mean laughter, had increased to where Arnold Palmer and his group was now looking back from the next tee trying to figure out what was going on. Something had spread through the crowd like a ripple on water to where everyone was laughing and straining to see what the heck happened.

Looking back toward the crowd, I tried to figure out what everyone was laughing about. Heck, I enjoyed a good laugh as well as the next guy. But everyone was looking at me. And what's more, everyone was laughing at me.

Then I suddenly realized the reason for all the laughter. Because of the pressure and the anger, I wasn't thinking right. Instead of taking off my right shoe and sock and stepping into the water with my right foot, I had taken off my left shoe and sock.

For those of you who haven't figured it out yet, my left foot was bone dry. So were my left shoe and sock for that matter. But my right pant leg, my right shoe and sock were soaked. You see, I had taken my shoe and sock off the wrong foot.

"Yeah, sure," my caddie said, "you'll be back in Reno in a couple of days, but I have to live in this town. I'll never live this one down."

Okay, it was embarrassing, sloshing my way up to the green while four or five thousand people fell down laughing, peeing their pants and all of that sort of stuff. Yeah, let's watch the guy playing behind Arnold. He's a comedian. A clown. A warm-up act for a Vegas show.

Damn, how embarrassing. But worst of all was my caddie. I got up to the green and noticed he was standing back, trying to be inconspicuous, almost hiding in the crowd. And, instead of handing me my putter, he flung it at me. He actually threw my putter across the green at me. And then, of course, I two-putted for par.

When my round was over, I tried to get off the eighteenth green and into the clubhouse as quickly as possible. Actually I was hoping my locker was big enough for one grown man to climb inside and hide out until everyone left.

However, waiting for me at the edge of the ropes was the little lady I had given the autograph to earlier. She patted me on the hand and whispered, "Robert, you're still my favorite person and actor. But I have a little advice. First of all, fire your caddie. He isn't very nice. And after that, quit golfing. Please, Robert, sell your clubs and make more movies. Please."

It goes without saying I never made it to Sunday. In fact, when I arrived at the clubhouse the next morning, I was told that a pro by the name of George Bayer talked his way in and with that, they moved the guy with the damp right foot out. So be it.

Driving back to Reno I cared about getting scratched from the tournament and yet I didn't care. Sure I wanted to hang in there and try to pick up a check on Sunday, but at the same time, I just wanted to get as far away from Palm Springs as I could.

Well, I did have one thing to fall back on and that was the knowledge every one of us have had our share of ups and downs, wins and losses. And when you get right down to it, I'll bet everyone has, at one time or another, gone out on the golf course and had the same kind of day. Yeah, I told myself in convincing fashion, I'm not the only guy in the world who stood in front of five thousand people and put the wrong foot in the water.

###

For Jim —
a double "Pro"
(as a player and
as a guy) — Thanks for being
So nice Always Jerry Lewis
7/31

Jerry Lewis, one of the great men of this world. It's a true honor to really get to know him. Thanks for being my friend.

7

America's Ambassador
Of Comedy

He was born Joseph Levitch in Newark, New Jersey, on March 16, 1926. His showbiz career actually started at the Stevenson Lake Hotel when he was only five years old. He went out on stage in front of a large audience and sang a song, *Brother Can You Spare A Dime*. He had a nice voice and was a cute little boy. The appreciative audience gave him a round of applause.

With his first performance in the books, he turned to walk offstage, but accidentally tripped in the light well. I guess it really must have been something to see – lights popping and a little kid stumbling. Suddenly, the audience was laughing, howling. At that instant, a second career was born, a career that would eventually give him the title of America's Ambassador of Comedy.

Later in life he would look back on that introduction to show business and explain the difference between the applause and the laughter. He said, the applause made him feel good. But the laughter he heard was awesome. The sound of an audience laughing was something he wanted to hear over and over again. He wanted to stumble onstage, trip in the light well so to speak, and make people laugh. He wanted to spend his life hearing the sound of laughter.

Image that, most of us would have been embarrassed... tripping in a light well and listening to the audience laugh at us. But this little boy was different. He was very special. You see, the laughter didn't embarrass him. The laughter was telling him to find another lightwell to stumble over. The laughter was telling him the reason he was in the world. He was born to be a comedian, born to make people laugh. Of course I'm talking about the often imitated but never surpassed, Jerry Lewis.

As far back as I can remember, I was always a Jerry Lewis fan. Sure it was Dean Martin and Jerry Lewis. And the truth was a person couldn't be a Jerry Lewis fan without liking Dean Martin. They were great! But Jerry was special. In my estimation there was just something about Jerry, his antics, his voice, the expressions, the make-up, the clumsy act made me laugh. I'm not talking about a few chuckles. I'm talking about laughing. Jerry Lewis made me and the world laugh.

It had nothing to do with being star-struck, but I did tell myself I would like to play a round of golf with Jerry Lewis someday. I thought he would not only be a fun guy but a good guy. And hey, considering the fact I was adding new clients from Hollywood to my list all the time, I felt there was a reasonable chance Jerry would eventually call for a lesson. Of course, more times than not, lessons had a way of moving from the practice range to the first tee. Yes, I would tell myself while watching Jerry in a movie or on television, someday, we'll tee it up and play a round of golf.

As I predicted, one day I received the phone call. The voice on the other end of the line identified himself as "Jerry Lewis."

Finally, I thought, Jerry heard about me and needed a lesson. Sure, we'd eventually tee it up on the course, but in the beginning, I was excited about giving Jerry a lesson.

"Mr. Chenoweth, I have a little problem," Jerry said.

Mr. Chenoweth. Jerry called me "Mr. Chenoweth." Jerry was no doubt showing a little respect for the man who could straighten out his golf game. It's wonderful to be needed.

Well, there was no doubt in my mind, Jerry had heard about me from some of my Hollywood students. His game was obviously suffering and he was coming to the ol' links doctor for the cure. But hey, I really didn't care what Jerry's problem was – hook or slice or even the yips, I certainly would do everything possible to straighten him out.

I was just about ready to blurt it all out. You know, to tell Jerry that when it came to golf, I had seen it all. Why with a little tweaking I'd have him straightened out in no time at all.

But something told me to just take it easy. In other words, don't break my arm trying to pat myself on the back while telling Jerry what a great instructor I was. What the heck, if Jerry was calling me, that meant someone else had already tooted my horn.

I backed off and let Jerry explain his problem.

Naturally, it turned out that Jerry was performing in Reno. And Jerry, typical of the entertainment crowd, brought his golf clubs. I knew exactly where Jerry was going because I had heard the story before. In fact that's how it always started. I'd get a call from a celebrity who was in town performing at one of the Casinos. The celebrity brought golf clubs but needed yours truly to cure a hook or slice or whatever. I understood.

Jerry was beating around the bush instead of getting to the crux of the problem. It sounded like he might have been a little embarrassed about having to call me. Boy, I thought... he must really have the yips or even the dreaded shanks.

Several times during the conversation I was ready to interrupt and tell Jerry not to worry. It didn't matter what his problem was because I had seen it all. But instead, I sat back and patiently let Jerry explain his reason for the phone call. And he did. However, he wasn't calling for a lesson. He was calling for a last-minute tee time.

A tee time, I thought. Wow. It was Sunday morning. I was booked solid and Jerry needed a tee time.

It turned out that Jerry and his friends went to Hidden Valley Country Club without a tee time. But Hidden Valley was having a tournament. So Jerry needed a place to play and my name was mentioned.

At the time, in addition to being Hollywood's golfing guru, I was also running Brookside Golf Course in Reno. It was a popular place and, of course, we were busy. I'm talking about packed solid. But this was Jerry Lewis, my favorite entertainer.

"Come on over and we'll get you out," I said. Maybe I wasn't going to give Jerry a lesson or even tee it up with him, but I was still going to meet the man.

About forty-five minutes later, Jerry and his group showed up. It was perfect timing. We had a last minute cancellation and the first tee was open. So, Jerry and his friends made a quick trip from the parking lot to the tee.

Suddenly it hit me. I told myself that just as soon as Jerry snapped his drive or faded it or dubbed it, the ol' Links Doctor would be there to offer some free advice. And, believe me, I was positive Jerry would hack up the first tee shot of the day. After all, he had just spent forty-five minutes crammed in an automobile driving to the course. Then there wasn't any time to hit a few range balls and loosen up. It was rush, rush, rush to the first tee and then hurry up and hit the ball.

"A big hook," I whispered to myself as Jerry prepared to hit his first drive. I wasn't wishing Jerry anything bad. I was just predicting a big hook. You see, I knew how hard it was to hit a good shot whenever I rushed. The toughest shot in golf is the first shot of the day. And if a person isn't warmed up and is being rushed, then the difficulty of the first shot is only going to be compounded. I was thinking if that kind of a situation was tough on me, a pro, then what chance did an amateur have?

Jerry would have to be a little quick with his swing. And once a person gets a little quick, the tendency is to hook the ball. So... just as soon as Jerry snapped one, I'd be there to help him out.

Slow and easy and about two hundred and sixty yards right down the middle. I'm talking about Jerry's first swing and the end result. It was a slow and easy swing and the ball traveled about two hundred and sixty yards right down the middle of the fairway.

"How's that for the first one of the day?" Jerry asked with a big grin.

"Well... it went forward," I said in a quiet, unemotional way. Hey, I was surprised. Jerry should have been quick with the swing and he was supposed to snap-hook one.

"It went forward," Jerry repeated and then laughed. "That's funny. The way you said it. That's funny."

Instead of making a little grip adjustment for Jerry, or telling him to swing slow and easy, I gave him and his group some different advice. "Have fun."

During days when the course was busy, I would usually go out in my golf cart and check on things. It was a combination of socializing and marshaling. In other words, I would drive around, say hello to the players, and diplomatically make sure everyone was keeping up with the group in front of them.

Several hours later, while making my tour, I spotted Jerry and his group on the sixteenth green. I drove up to them and we made some small talk on the way to the next tee. That's when Jerry asked me to join them for the last two holes.

"I'd love to," I said. "But I'm in my loafers and I don't have clubs."

"I've played in loafers before and as for clubs, use mine," Jerry said as he tossed me a golf ball.

It was an offer I couldn't refuse.

From the very beginning, Jerry made me feel comfortable. I felt as though we had been friends for a long time. There was a little bit of kidding and joking around and then it was time for me to hit one. My first tee shot was dead, solid perfect and from there it only got better. I finished seventeen and eighteen birdie, birdie. I'm talking about two easy birdies. Why they were such easy birdies that Jerry and his friends were really impressed. I tried to act casual, but even I was a little surprised. Not that I hadn't birdied seventeen and eighteen before, but today I did it wearing loafers, using someone elses clubs and a putter I had never seen before. Maybe that would be my approach for the next tournament I played in – borrow Jerry's clubs and play in loafers.

Those two holes of golf ended much too quickly. And after it was over, Jerry was pressed for time and had to leave. But at least I could say that I had met and played golf with Jerry Lewis. And, he was, just as I suspected, a terrific guy. Oh, he wasn't the Jerry Lewis we all saw and loved in the movies. You know, the stumble bum. In fact, he was a terrific athlete and a very good stick. He could play golf, and he sure knew how to have fun. But when it was over, I thought it was over. I figured Jerry would go his way and I'd go mine. I just didn't think his game needed any major surgery by the Links Doctor.

The next morning, I showed up for work at my typical time: dawn. The sun was inching over the far eastern horizon as I pulled into the parking lot, got out of my car and started to walk toward the club house. Then I spotted another car in the parking lot with a man sitting in the front seat. For a second I thought it was Jerry Lewis. I took a closer look. He sure looked like Jerry Lewis.

I went over to the car. Yep, it was Jerry Lewis. He was drinking coffee and reading the newspaper.

I knocked on the window and Jerry looked up. He smiled, rolled down the window and accused me of keeping "banker's hours."

"Banker's hours!" I replied. "I'm the first one here! It's the crack of dawn."

Jerry engaged in a monologue which seemed to offer fragments of evidence he was an early riser. But while Jerry was talking I had the impression he never went to bed. He said something about working late, getting cleaned up, having an early breakfast and then driving over to the course. I never heard anything about bed and sleep.

Several years later, after I really got to know Jerry, I would come to understand that my first impression about his sleeping habits were much more accurate than his explanation of being an early riser. Heck, Jerry wasn't an early riser. I don't think he ever went to bed. He never stopped working. It was twenty-four hours a day, work, work and more work. He was a workaholic who might have taken a catnap once in a while, but certainly not an early riser.

Well, that's how it began, my friendship with Jerry... in the parking lot of a golf course at six in the morning. He probably hadn't been to bed and I really was an early riser. I was an early-to-bed guy, too. But there we were, at the crack of dawn when Jerry said, "Jim, I want to learn how to golf... I want to be able to swing a club just like you."

I started teaching Jerry the finer points of the game, but in all honesty I never gave Jerry a normal lesson. We hardly ever spent any time on the driving range. Jerry wasn't interested in typical lessons. He learned by watching. We'd go out on the course, I'd swing the club, hit a particular shot and Jerry would duplicate exactly what he saw. It was remarkable because Jerry could watch me do something one time, and he had the ability to pull off the same shot.

We started our relationship as golfing buddies but soon became friends. And as our friendship was growing, I found a sadness in it all. You see, there were millions of Jerry Lewis fans, but only a few of us would ever have the privilege of meeting the man and being able to spent quality time with him.

Just mention the name Jerry Lewis and people will smile or laugh. And sure, Jerry made the world laugh, but sadly the world will probably never realize the depth, character and beauty of my friend Jerry Lewis.

I know a lot of people say it and most of us believe it. I'm talking about that stuff where we're all said to be equal. Well, maybe we all come into this world the same way, but believe me, we are not equal.

Listen to the music of Mozart and tell me we're all the same. Read about the life of Gandhi and tell me we're all equal. You see, I just happen to believe that some of the people who travel through this world are special. For some reason, call it Divine Intervention or whatever, but there are special people in this world and Jerry Lewis is one of them.

I don't want to embarrass Jerry with this little passage because he usually just goes about his daily routines without a lot of fanfare. But I have been among the privileged few who have come to really get to know Jerry. And seriously, he is a very special person. Just ask those little children suffering with muscular dystrophy or their parents, and they'll tell you Jerry is special.

Okay, we all know that once a year Jerry goes on a twenty-four hour crusade, a telethon aimed at raising money for the Muscular Dystrophy Foundation. God bless Jerry for that effort. But not many folks understand that MD is more than a one day a year effort in the life of Jerry Lewis. I've been there when Jerry would get a call about one of his little children being sick... real sick and dying. A person would have to be there to understand how those calls would impact Jerry. His heart would be torn out. His eyes would well with tears. He would cry.

I'm reminded of the story when Jerry received one of those calls. Immediately, he dropped what he was doing, drove to the airport and purchased a ticket. Jerry was going to Texas.

It turned out that one of Jerry's Kids, one of the kids who was on a recent telethon, was dying. The little boy wanted to see Jerry one more time. They said the little boy was fighting to stay alive because he wanted to see Jerry one more time. And so the little boy's parents called and Jerry granted that last wish.

At the hospital, Jerry softly touched his hand against the little boy's cheek and said, "Now you can go to sleep."

Yes, it's like I said, Jerry Lewis is a good man, a generous man with a big heart, a very special man.

There are many times when I sit back and travel that worn path over those memories, beautiful memories of a wonderful friendship. I'm reminded of the time when the crooked politics of Reno's City Council cost me my job at Brookside Golf Course. But suddenly Jerry was there when I needed him most.

My association with Brookside Golf Course began when the original developers simply couldn't make it work. They were losing money and sliding down the slippery slope toward bankruptcy. I was hired and in no time at all business had increased tenfold. But it was too little too late.

The golf course property was owned by the City of Reno. And just when everything seemed it would work out, the City stepped in and took over the operations. Suddenly I found myself working for some character who must have studied an Al Capone business manual. I'm talking about a certain member of Reno's City Council. I'm talking about the kind of guy who should have been fingerprinted, stripped searched, and given a prominent place in the Post Office for his photograph to be displayed.

It was well-known and publicized fact that Reno had some rather corrupt members of the City Council back in those days. I never realized how corrupt until one of the Council's seediest members paid me a friendly visit.

"Can we talk?" the greasy-looking man asked.

"Sure," I answered with one hand on my wallet and the other hand holding the cash drawer to the register.

"Not here," Mr. Grease said. "We gotta' talk in private. In your office. I gots some stuff I wanna show you."

At the time, I really didn't understand. So, we went into my office and Mr. Grease closed the door. He glanced around the room like a nervous rat looking for a swooping hawk. Then he gave me one of those Humphry Bogart shoulder moves and asked, "If you're standing outsides the door can you hear whats we gots to say insides this room?"

"I don't know," I answered in a serious tone. "I've never stood outside the door listening to myself talking in here."

Mr. Grease gave me a dirty look. I don't think he appreciated my humor. He continued. "Okay, Chenoweth, he's the deal."

Mr. Grease produced a file from under his arm, spread some papers on my desk and said, "Now, your contract is up the first of the year and if you wanna a job wit' me, then it'll cost you. And to be sure there's no funny business, I want you to know I checked what's been goin' on here. I know what you're rakin' in and I want ten percent every month. Not nine percent. Ten percent. And I mean ten percent of everything."

Mr. Grease had all the numbers from the driving range, green fees, carts, food, beverage, and sales in the pro shop. It was all there in black and white. He knew exactly how much the course was *rakin' in* and he wanted ten percent of everything.

Gee, I thought. It all sounds fair to me.

My first reaction was to look around the office for the camera. This had to be a stunt for *Candid Camera*. Alan Funt had sneaked into my office, set up a hidden camera, and was filming my reaction to being confronted by a make-believe, slimy, nefarious, sinister, evil, wicked, criminal element from the City Council. It all had to be staged. It was a natural – the honest, hard-working club pro eking out a living... the fat, greasy shakedown artist breaking the law.

But there were two problems with that particular theory. First of all, there wasn't any place for Alan Funt to hide his camera in my office. And secondly, Mr. Grease really sounded serious.

"Ten percent," Mr. Grease repeated. "Ten percent of everything, every month and I want it in cash. Understand?"

I understood, all right. This wasn't *Candid Camera*. This was real! But why stop at only ten percent?

I stood up and told Mr. Grease, "Instead of ten percent, I'm going to give you one hundred percent... Okay?"

"One hundred percent," he repeated in a voice that sounded a little perplexed. Obviously he didn't understand my generous offer.

"Yeah," I said. "One hundred percent. I'm going to give you the entire one hundred percent of a *%$# beating unless you get your fat, &%$#, greasy $#@& out of my office."

"Hey, hey!" Mr. Grease rebutted me. "I'm jus' tryin' to be fair. Ten percent ain't that much when you consider your job's at stake. Remember, your contract is up the first of the year and if you want it renewed, you better pay up or else."

For a fat, greasy character he slid out of my office rather quickly. In fact, before I could get around the desk and keep my promise of giving him one hundred percent of a beating, he had gathered up his paper work and bolted from the building.

During days of garlic, gunpowder and gangrene, Al Capone could use those type of strong-arm tactics in order to feed his criminal empire. But this was not the Roaring Twenties and it wasn't Chicago and I wouldn't be intimidated by a two-bit crook. What would Mr. Grease do? Get his buddies to machine gun my golf cart? Ha.

I laughed the entire incident off. And why wouldn't I? I felt my future was secure because golfers and non-golfers alike knew I was an honest man doing a good job. So, I never took Mr. Grease's threat seriously. When he scurried out of my office like an over stuffed rat, I thought that would be the end of it.

However, true to his word, Mr. Grease went on a campaign to get me ousted. Still, I felt I was on firm ground. After all, I was a hard-working, honest man who had turned the golf course around. What's more, we were showing a profit. But the City Council didn't renew my contract and suddenly I was on the outside looking in.

The regulars at Brookside fought for me, but it didn't do any good. I wasn't going to pay anyone under the table and that meant I wasn't going to work at a golf course owned by the City of Reno.

Shortly after I was removed from Brookside, I received a phone call from Jerry Lewis. "Jim," he said, "Get on the next plane to Vegas."

I had received those type of calls from Jerry before. There were times when Jerry was scheduled to play in a tournament and he'd call me to pack his bag or just to travel with him. Other times, Jerry would want a playing lesson and I'd hear that familiar voice say, "I need you. Get your clubs. Let's go." And in the past, I would always drop whatever I was doing and go. But today I couldn't leave.

I didn't want to tell Jerry my problems. But I couldn't leave home at a time like this even if I wanted to. I was looking for a job. My life was in turmoil. I had a family. So, I made some lame excuse as to why I couldn't come to Vegas.

But Jerry said, "Jim, I need you. I really need you to get on the next plane and meet someone. It's important. I'm counting on you."

I bid my wife and family good-bye, and jumped on the next plane south. Still, I didn't know what it was about, but Jerry wanted me to meet a Mr.

Jess Hinkle at the Sahara Hotel. Jerry said to be there at 10:00 a.m. sharp. Well, I was there on time, but Jerry was running late.

Jess Hinkle was an executive with the Del Web Corporation. And, I might add that Jess was a terrific guy. We talked about golf and golf courses. We even talked a little about Jerry Lewis. But I still didn't know what the meeting was about and by now, Jerry was really running late. It was 10:30. It wasn't like Jerry to be late.

I was beginning to feel a little like the odd man out. You see, it's like I've already mentioned. I just didn't know what to say, because I still didn't have any idea what this meeting was all about. And where was Jerry?

After a few more minutes of Jess having this one-sided conversation, he took a key off his desk, stood up and said, "Come on, I guess you want to get to work."

Work? I still didn't understand.

We walked up the hall to a door. Jess slid the key into the lock, opened the door and said, "Well, Jim. Here's your new office. Jerry wanted it to be a surprise for you."

I was speechless. Somehow, Jerry Lewis had learned that I lost my job at Brookside Golf Course. And now, because of Jerry Lewis, I was the new Executive Director of Golf for Del Web Hotels International.

I walked into my new office, sat down at my desk and nearly cried. The entire ordeal of fighting with City Council and losing my job had placed a tremendous amount of stress on my wife and family. And now, because of Jerry, I had a new job.

Jerry Lewis fans throughout the world know him because of his movies, television work and the Muscular Dystrophy Foundation. But only a privileged few really know the true depth and compassion of the man.

I tried to call Jerry. I wanted to thank him. But he was off somewhere traveling the world. No one seemed to know where I could get in touch with him. Thank you would have to wait for another day.

Over the years I attempted to condition myself to expect the unexpected with Jerry. But it never worked because Jerry was so unpredictable. Jerry had a sense of timing, a perfect sense of timing whereby I would get blown away by his kindness and generosity.

I'm reminded of the time when Jerry and I were supposed to play an early round of golf. And I do mean early. Jerry was an *early riser*. Remember?

It was still dark as I drove through the deserted streets toward the golf course. In another hour or so the sun would be up. But... by that time, Jerry and I would have already played three or four holes. Yes, Jerry liked to get an early start.

Suddenly, my car conked out. I pulled over to the curb, and tried to get it started. The engine just wouldn't turn over.

Since the Oldsmobile dealership didn't keep Jerry's hours, I couldn't call the service department. Instead, I found a pay phone, called my wife, apologized for waking her at such an ungodly hour, and then explained my dilemma. Telling her where the car was, I asked if she would call the Oldsmobile dealership when it opened for business. That way, I could get the car towed in and repaired while I played a round of golf.

Arriving at the golf course in a taxi, I found Jerry in the dark parking lot waiting for me. Jerry's clubs were already on his golf cart and he was nervously pacing. He had been ready to go for nearly an hour.

Quickly, Jerry took my clubs out of the cab, put them on the cart and while we drove to the first tee, I explained what had happened. Jerry didn't say much other than I should get a dependable car.

Later, that afternoon, the telephone rang and I answered. It was the Cadillac dealership calling. A pleasant voice said, "Mr. Chenoweth, your car is ready to be picked up."

Jerry playing the straight man and me wearing the clown pants.

I hung up the phone and suddenly it hit me. Cadillac? What gives here? I told my wife to call the Oldsmobile dealership and have them pick up the car.

My wife insisted that she did call the Olds dealership and they did pick up the car. However, I was positive the Cadillac dealership had just called and said my car was ready.

The first phone call I made was to the Olds dealership. The service manager said to hold for a minute and he would check on the status of my car. He was gone for quite a while and when he came back, he said he hadn't located my car just yet. He'd call back.

In the meantime, I phoned the Cadillac dealership and asked if they had my car. They did. At least they had a car owned by a Mr. Jim Chenoweth. But something was wrong. The car in question was a Cadillac and I owned an Oldsmobile.

"But I don't own a Cadillac," I told the lady at the dealership.

"Oh, but you do own a Cadillac," she answered. "I'm looking at it right now."

Something strange was happening because the lady informed me that a Jim Chenoweth owned a Cadillac. And furthermore, that Jim Chenoweth had the same address as me.

I thought about the situation for a moment and came up with a logical assumption. Obviously, the Olds dealership couldn't fix my car. Perhaps they needed a special part or something like that. So they took it across the street to the Caddy dealer. And then, at the Cadillac dealership, some clerk messed up all the paper work. Yes, I said to myself, somehow my name and address ended up on the title to a Cadillac. I know it all sounds like I was reaching on this one, but that was the only thing that made any sense.

We got in my wife's car and drove downtown. Walking into the show-room of the Cadillac dealership, the manager came up to me and said,

"We got her all ready, Mr. Chenoweth. All you have to do is sign the papers." The manager pointed to a brand new Caddy parked right in front of the showroom.

I was totally lost. "There has to be some mistake. My Oldsmobile was brought in for repairs... I think... and all of a sudden you're trying to sell me a new car."

The sales manager smiled and replied, "I don't know anything about repairs to your other car. But I can assure you the Cadillac is very much yours. All you have to do is sign the papers and drive the car home. Mr. Lewis has already written the check. He paid for it."

That's the way it was with Jerry. I just never knew what to expect. During our round of golf he made a quiet statement about me having a dependable car. Then he went out and bought me one.

My wife fell in love with the car. I fell in love with the car. Why wouldn't we? It was a beautiful automobile. But... we couldn't keep it. Oh, don't get me wrong, because I did appreciate Jerry's kindness. But I couldn't keep such an expensive gift.

Over the years I gradually learned to be real careful about what I said around Jerry. It took me a while to understand, but sometimes even casual conversation would open the flood gates of Jerry's generosity.

I remember one time Jerry did some work for Oreo cookies, I think. Or maybe someone just sent him a case or two of Oreo cookies. At any rate, we were having some Oreo cookies and a glass of milk when I said, "These cookies sure are good."

A week later the UPS truck pulled up to my home with two cases of Oreos. I had enough Oreos to feed everyone in the State of Nevada and then some.

Another time, I made a comment about Jerry's cologne. It was called Dunhill. I think Jerry picked it up in England. All I said was that his cologne had a nice fragrance and several weeks later, UPS was at my home delivering a case of Dunhill.

After receiving my lifetime supply of Dunhill, I exercised extreme caution whenever having casual dialogue with Jerry. It wasn't that I didn't appreciate the gifts, because I did. And it wasn't that I didn't enjoy opening presents because I did. But with Jerry having a tendency to make every day Christmas, I didn't want anyone to think I was taking advantage of his generosity. And believe me, Jerry was generous, a very generous man.

Speaking of generous, I'm reminded of a day when we played a round of golf and were sitting in the clubhouse afterwards having a drink. Jerry leaned across the table, touched a medal I was wearing and asked, "What's this?"

"A Saint Christopher medal," I answered.

"I know that," Jerry said. "I mean what's this?" Jerry was pointing at the silver chain.

The medal was a gift from my wife. During the course of daily activity, I broke the chain. Actually I broke the chain about a year or so ago. Instead of taking it to a jeweler, I fixed it myself with a piece of wire. Since I have more thumbs than fingers, the repair job to the chain looked a little bush league.

Jerry called it, "Tacky. Jim, that's tacky. Real tacky."

Okay, my repair job wasn't the best. But, I'd get the chain fixed one of these days.

That night I was rousted from bed by the ringing telephone. I sat up and glanced at the clock. It was midnight. "Gee," I looked at the phone and asked, "I wonder who's calling me at midnight?"

I picked up the phone and said, "Jerry, it's midnight. Some of us really are early risers."

Whenever Jerry was playing in town my phone could ring at any hour of the night. Even when Jerry wasn't playing in town my phone could ring at any hour. But midnight, by Jerry's standards, was a respectable time to be calling me.

"Get over here," the voice said. "I have something I want you to see."

"But, Jerry. I've seen the show a hundred times or more. I'm tired. That's why I went to bed several hours ago."

That was a very true and accurate statement. I had seen Jerry's show at least a hundred times and I did go to bed because I was tired. But Jerry was Jerry and wouldn't take no for an answer.

"I don't want you to see the show. I have something else I want you to see. It's important... So, come on over. Okay?"

Arriving at the Sahara, I went into Jerry's dressing room. He was changing clothes, getting ready for another show. Jerry looked at me and said, "Over there. On the mirror. What do you see?"

There was a large mirror in Jerry's dressing room. The mirror was sort of his personal calendar, a date book so-to-speak of appointments along with names and phone numbers of friends. I'm talking about a place where Jerry taped up little pieces of paper to remind him of everything and anything. To this day I'm still not sure how Jerry ever found anything on his bulletin board. It was simply a cluttered mess.

I looked at the mirror for a moment. I didn't understand. But this was, of course, Jerry Lewis. And, it's like I said. Over the years I had come to expect the unexpected. Still, I didn't have a clue as to what I was looking for or at.

Finally, Jerry asked, "Don't you see it?"

"See what?"

"Are you blind, Chenoweth? Up in the top left-hand corner... Can't you see it?"

Following Jerry's instructions, my eyes moved toward the top left-hand corner of the mirror. And there, admidst the clutter of notes, I saw a small box, a gift wrapped box taped to the mirror – gold paper and a red ribbon.

"It's for you," Jerry said while tying his shoes.

I reached for the box and thought, it's Christmas morning again, another wonderful Christmas morning.

Opening the box and I saw a Saint Christopher medal, a golden medal and chain. It was beautiful, and expensive. I'm not saying it was as costly as the Cadillac, but it was an expensive piece of jewelry.

I looked at Jerry. His expression told it all. For the first time I realized how much he loved sharing his good fortune with other people. I knew that giving me this gift meant a lot to Jerry. But it also meant a lot to me.

"Jerry, I'll think about you and what our friendship means to me everytime I look at this medal. Thank you."

What began as a round of golf had become a warm and wonderful friendship. Actually I felt more like family than a friend. That was the wonderful thing about Jerry. He made me feel like a member of his family. And believe me, family was always first and foremost in Jerry's life.

Make no mistake about it. Jerry loved his wife and sons, but there was always a special place in his heart for friends. He had a profound sense of loyalty to family and friends and I think it had to do with his childhood.

Jerry was born in Newark, New Jersey, and was the son of show business people. His parents were always on the road, and because of that, Jerry spent most of his youth with relatives – mainly his grandmother, Sarah. It wasn't a bad childhood but rather a lonely one.

Some people might find it surprising to discover the most special times I ever spent with Jerry were not on the golf course or watching the UPS man bring large boxes up to my doorstep. It was those moments when he would get nostalgic and reminisce about his childhood.

With great fondness Jerry would talk about those summers, those occasions when he would join his parents in the Catskills where they were performing in the resorts of the Borscht Circuit. But whenever Jerry mentioned those times, I could tell they were too far and few between to suit him. Yes, he loved his grandmother, but he missed his mother and father. He missed being a family.

There were times when I would listen to Jerry talk about his childhood, and then go home and cry. As a man, Jerry made the world laugh. But as a child he sometimes traveled a very lonely and sad journey.

I'm reminded of the time when Jerry shared one of his saddest, most humiliating experiences of early life with me. He was ten years old and in grade school. It was the last day of class. School was about to recess for the summer. Normally it would have been a time of great expectation, a time when the final bell would signal the beginning of those warm days and wonderful nights of total freedom. But this day of anticipation would soon become a nightmare in the life of Jerry, a haunting memory he would carry forever.

The teacher began to read the names of the children in the classroom. When their name was read, the teacher had them get up from their desk and stand against the blackboard. One by one the teacher read names from her list. And as instructed, once their name was called, they would get up and stand along the blackboard. Surely, Jerry thought, everyone's name would be eventually called. But what did all of this mean?

Finally, with the children standing and staring at the lone survivor of role call, the teacher explained what was about to happen. The children standing had been promoted to the next grade. They were about to be escorted to their new classroom. However, anyone whose name hadn't been called, anyone who remained seated, had failed and would occupy the same seat in this same classroom next year. Everyone except Jerry was moving on.

I think a part of Jerry's heart was forever lost in the classroom on that particular day. And when Jerry told me that story, I thought, my God, wasn't there a better way for a teacher to treat this little boy? What was the reason for public humiliation?

Needless to say, Jerry wasn't enamored with the classroom. He quit high school after only one year and moved out into the real world. Jerry had a dream, a dream he dared to dream many years ago as a five-year-old little boy stumbling across the stage. He wanted to be an entertainer, an entertainer who would make people laugh.

Even at the young age of sixteen, Jerry was already a veteran of the entertainment business. He had spent many summers traveling and performing on stage with his parents. But now, he was out on his own and little did he know that he would struggle for many years in order to become an overnight sensation.

Jerry moved to New York City and began making the round of booking agents. And his act was typical Jerry Lewis – zany and hilarious. The records of a famous singer would play backstage while Jerry stood in front of the audience mimicking the song and the entertainer.

By the age of eighteen, Jerry's life would change dramatically. He had fallen in love, and soon afterwards married Patty Palmer, a vocalist with the Jimmy Dorsey band. To support his wife, he picked up odd jobs working as a soda jerk, a shipping clerk, and a theater usher. He also continued his entertainment career and found rather steady employment working summers in the Catskills. But life was a daily struggle because Jerry, as yet, hadn't found the magic formula that would transform the years of hard work into an overnight success story.

Finally, in 1946, it happened. While making the rounds in New York City, Jerry met another struggling, small-time entertainer, a baritone from Stubenville, Ohio, by the name of Dean Martin. Dean could sing. He was handsome. But like Jerry, Dean couldn't find steady work.

Shortly after meeting Dean, Jerry had an engagement playing at the 500 Club in Atlantic City. When a singer came down ill, Jerry told management about Dean Martin. But management wanted more than just another singer. And in that instant of time, Martin and Lewis was born. For here was the inspiration which would label Jerry Lewis and Dean Martin as overnight successes.

"But he is more than just a singer," Jerry said. "We do an act together. A comedy routine."

Of course, nothing was further from the truth. Jerry and Dean had played in the same clubs and were becoming friends, but they had never worked together. However, before the night was over, they would take their first steps toward becoming two of the most recognizable entertainers in the world.

During the first show of the night, Jerry did his routine and made the audience laugh. When he was finished Dean came on stage and sang. But between shows, management paid Martin and Lewis a visit. Management wanted to see their act. So, Dean Martin and Jerry Lewis would do "their" act or else be thrown out of the joint. With little or no time to plan or rehearse, Jerry and Dean walked out on stage together at the 500 Club for the first time. Amazingly, the act was vintage Martin and Lewis. Dean sang and Jerry continually interrupted him. Spontaneous ad-libbing, coupled with clowning and the trading of insults, it was the beginning of a ten-year span where they would become the number-one stars of stage, radio, TV, and motion pictures. Whereas they were struggling as singles in the entertainment business, they had become overnight sensations as an act.

During those ten glory years, Jerry and Dean played in all the major clubs throughout the United States as well as the many stages of the world. They also made seventeen movies, movies that were extremely successful financially. But on July 26, 1956, the ten-year anniversary of their first performance in the 500 Club, it was over. Jerry Lewis and Dean Martin went their separate ways.

Shortly afterwards, Jerry began producing his own films. Often snubbed and never taken seriously by American critics, Jerry took his films to France where he became an icon. Although comedy was Jerry's genre, he was nonetheless praised by serious critics as *Le Roi du Crazy*. Even the *Cahiers du Cinema* and *Positif*, two of the most prestigious film publications in France, which more often than not differed in their critical philosophy, had been overwhelming unanimous in their praise of Jerry's genius.

With Jerry's popularity and work standing the test of time, he came to Paris in 1971 and played to 16 sell-out crowds in the Olympia. It was nothing less than standing ovations and appreciative cheers, a tribute reserved for only the greatest entertainers. From the little boy who once dared to dream about making people laugh, Jerry had expanded his horizons to a place in time where he was making the audiences of the world laugh.

We all know and love Jerry as a comedian, but I think one of his greatest performances came in a movie with Robert De Niro called *The King of Comedy*. It seemed a fitting title for an actor/comedian of Jerry's talents. However, instead of playing the part of a comedian, Jerry played a straight man, and De Niro was the struggling and wacky comedian. But here, Jerry showed the world his great depth as an actor. Jerry's performance won him critical acclaim throughout the world.

Jerry Lewis. What can I say? There are times when I look at the guy sitting in the golf cart next to me, and I have to shake my head and marvel at the places he has seen and the things he has accomplished. And yet, when Jerry and I are out on the course or he's sleeping on my sofa after dinner, I see a regular sort of a guy and a good friend. Oh, don't get me wrong, because Jerry can get a little zany even in regular life. But for the most part, Jerry is simply one of the boys.

Speaking of zany, I remember the time my phone rang and Jerry wanted me to fly to California for a tournament. Flip Wilson was having a two-day charity affair at La Costa, just north of San Diego. Jerry said he needed me. After a few minutes of conversation, I learned the tournament was strictly for amateurs. No pros. But Jerry wanted me to play in the practice round and spend a little time tweaking his swing.

It's like I mentioned before, Jerry's game never needed much tweaking. Oh, from time to time we would hit a few balls at the range and talk about the swing. But for the most, Jerry and I would usually head for the first tee and his lessons amounted to nothing more than him watching my swing and duplicating it.

"Okay, Jerry, I'll be there."

Later that afternoon I landed in San Diego. I picked up my clubs and suitcase at the luggage claim and went outside to find my ride to La Costa. That's when I noticed the commotion. I could see traffic was jammed and the crowd outside of the airport was laughing about something or someone. It must have really been entertaining, because everyone was howling. Then I heard a lady in the crowd say, "That is Jerry Lewis. Isn't it?"

Well... yes, it was Jerry Lewis.

Jerry was always a first-class guy. That meant Jerry would have a limousine waiting for me. But there wasn't a limo! Instead, I saw a big, black Rolls Royce angled against the curb. I had seen the Rolls before. It was Jerry's. And naturally, there was the chauffeur clad in a black suit, high boots, cap, and carrying a big sign which read: Mr Chenoweth. If you haven't guessed it by now, then let me continue. The chauffeur was Jerry. Oh, I'm not talking about my normal friend and golfing buddy, Jerry Lewis. I'm talking about the actor, the comedian, the wacky Jerry

Lewis. Here he was, wearing a chauffeur's uniform, complete with big, thick, coke-bottle glasses, fake teeth and running around the crowd carrying the sign looking for Mr. Chenoweth. Hey, it was funny stuff... funnier if you're not Mr. Chenoweth.

I tried to be inconspicuous. But how does a guy get into a big Rolls Royce with Jerry Lewis playing the part of a chauffeur and not be conspicuous?

Jerry opened the door and handed me a drink. Wow, first class. Then he took my clubs and suitcase and literally threw everything into the trunk. The crowd was falling down on the sidewalk laughing. I closed the door of the Rolls and thanked God for tinted windows.

Most of the participants in the tournament stayed at the La Costa Resort. But not Jerry. Instead, he had rented a big home that overlooked the golf course. After all, Jerry's friend, Mr. Chenoweth was coming to the tournament and they needed a little extra room. Well, Jerry had room... or should I say rooms – six bedrooms, a living room, rec room, dining room, television room, kitchen and eight bathrooms. It was at least 10, maybe 12,000 square feet of room. The home was so big that Jerry and I used a telephone to communicate.

That night Jerry told me I was in for a real treat. He had gone to the grocery store, spent $480.00 and was preparing dinner for his old golfing buddy, Mr. Chenoweth. Jerry had enough food in the kitchen to feed all the Marines stationed up the road at Camp Pendelton. But Jerry told me, "A little extra food is better than not enough."

I had to agree. When a person has company over for dinner, it is best to have a little extra than not enough. But Jerry's idea of a "little extra" meant that he and I would have enough food to survive the next ice age.

With all the talk about food, I realized I was hungry. But Jerry wouldn't let me snack. He didn't want me to spoil my appetite. After all, this dinner was going to be a "real treat."

As Jerry was talking about an old, secret recipe he had for baked chicken, I stood in the kitchen watching him work. I could have sworn Jerry said, "baked chicken." But he had a frying pan heating up on top of the stove. Since I was positive I had heard the words "baked chicken," I had to ask Jerry about the frying pan.

Jerry answered with a question. "What other way is there to bake a chicken?"

I pointed toward the oven and attempted to explain how it worked. But Jerry brushed it off by saying, "I never heard of such a thing."

"Well..." I said. "I guess it's all the same. To bake a cake or bake a chicken, just heat up the old frying pan on top of the stove and presto! There you have it! Baked cake or baked chicken."

When Jerry agreed with me about baking chicken in a frying pan on top of the stove, I knew his secret recipe would never threaten the enterprises of Colonel Sanders. Something told me that this dinner just wasn't going to be in the finger licking good category.

I have to admit, Jerry did a real nice job of cleaning up the whole chicken. Then he dropped it in the frying pan. Isn't that how the great chefs of the world bake a chicken?

I've heard some folks say that first-class service at a restaurant can help to make up for the blunders of the chef. I am here to dispute that.

When I say Jerry waited on me hand and foot, I mean he waited on me hand and foot. It was the best candle-light service in the history of service. Jerry kept a small towel draped over his arm. He continually filled my glass with water and brushed the crumbs away with a little whisk broom. Jerry saw to it that we even had real linen napkins, real silver, bone china, and the best bottle of wine money could buy. But all the first-class service in the world wasn't going to diminish the fact that Jerry had transformed that innocent chicken into something its own mother wouldn't have recognized. After Jerry finished frying his baked chicken, I could have taken it to forensic experts or a DNA lab for testing and there would be no evidence of it ever being a chicken.

Jerry was so proud of his baked chicken that I just couldn't bring myself to tell him the truth. It wasn't fit for human consumption. Heck, I wasn't sure a starving rat would consider it food. So, I heaped the vegetables on my plate and made short work of the bread. But as for the carcass of Jerry's "real treat," of course, I raved about how wonderful it looked, and I said it was delicious as I pretended to eat. Ugh!

Fortunately, the burning candles weren't that bright. So, Jerry didn't notice that my neatly folded linen napkin now contained something which was once a chicken's leg. But Jerry, sooner or later would figure everything out. I had to get rid of the evidence. All of the evidence.

"Bread. I'll go into the kitchen and get us some more bread," I said knowing full well that Jerry would cater to my every whim.

"No, no," Jerry said. "Just stay there. I'll get it."

Earlier, we had opened the dining room doors which lead to a large, redwood deck. And suddenly, just as Jerry turned and walked toward the kitchen, the mangled and charred remains of his baked chicken flew out of the dining room, over the deck and landed somewhere on the golf course below.

Hey, I don't like to brag, but I was a pretty fair baseball player in my day. That so-called baked chicken of Jerry's was the best fast ball I had ever thrown. Maybe, just maybe the coyotes living in the canyons around La Costa were hungry and dumb enough to eat that *thing*, but I wasn't.

Several moments later, when Jerry returned with the bread, he found me sitting back in the chair, rubbing my tummy, pretending I had polished off the whole chicken. "Delicious, Jerry. Simply delicious," I said.

Jerry looked at the empty plate and asked, "You ate it all? All of it?"

For some reason I honestly felt that Jerry was shocked that I or anyone would eat the chicken. But continuing to play the game I said, "All of it. I ate every delicious little morsel."

"You ate the bones, too?" Jerry asked with a suspicious expression on his face.

Sliding my chair back from the table, I simply ignored Jerry's last question. I stood up and said, "Nothing like a little nap to top off a great meal."

Just as I was turning to walk away, I noticed Jerry looked toward the dining room doors. No doubt about it. Jerry knew the fate of his baked chicken. But he never said a word. And that was because deep down inside Jerry had to know the truth. I was doing both of us a big favor. No one, not because of pride or starvation, should ever be expected to eat Jerry's baked-fried chicken. No one.

That night I didn't get much sleep. I tossed and turned. I was having nightmares about giant chickens. It was horrible. Every time I turned around, I saw a chicken holding a frying pan.

Suddenly, something was there, in my dark bedroom, standing beside me. This wasn't a bad dream. Quickly I sat up and focused my eyes on the shadowy figure beside my bed. It was Jerry. He was in his underwear holding a bed tray. He was serving me breakfast in bed.

"Breakfast!" I shouted while glancing at the clock. "It's four in the morning."

"Come on, Chenoweth. Get up," Jerry said. "The golf course is waiting for us. Now, eat your breakfast and let's go."

I sat up and thought, breakfast in bed. Hey, it wasn't a bad idea. With my dinner consisting mainly of bread and water, I woke to hunger pangs. Then I looked at my breakfast. Suddenly, I wasn't hungry.

Unbelievable, but with Jerry's idea of breakfast staring me in the face, I suddenly found myself wishing we would have saved a little of his baked-fried chicken from last night. Jerry called the concoction poached eggs. But eggs were never intended to looked like that.

As Jerry was walking out of the room I had to ask, "Jerry, what do you have against chickens?"

I don't think anyone is going to be too surprised to read that Jerry and I were the first ones to arrive at the driving range that morning. It wasn't all bad because we found a few balls near the base of the fence. We practiced chipping... in the dark. And, about two hours later, the fellow who took care of the range showed up for work.

"Boy," the range attendant said. "I didn't think anyone would be here yet. What'd you guys do, spend the night here?"

"Not quite," I answered while getting Jerry and I a couple baskets of balls.

Setting the baskets of range balls beside our clubs, Jerry said he wanted to watch me hit the driver. Hit the driver, I thought. I wasn't warmed up yet. And besides, I was hungry. And why wouldn't I be hungry. After all, I didn't have much of a dinner last night. And then this morning, I never told Jerry, but my breakfast was accidentally flushed down the toilet.

"I'm hungry, Jerry. Let's get something to eat."

"You can't be hungry," Jerry insisted. "You hogged up all the chicken last night, and had a big breakfast before leaving the house. Now, hit the driver. I want to see you hit the driver."

"Okay, I'll hit the driver."

I pulled the driver out of my bag, and took off the head cover. But something was smeared all over the head of the club. It looked like mustard. After a closer look, I came to the conclusion it was mustard. If mustard was smeared all over my driver, then there had to be a reason why my head cover felt heavy. And, all be darn, there was.

I glared at Jerry. Then, in a slow and deliberate tone I said, "Someone stuffed a hot dog smeared with mustard in my head cover. And, it looks like a kosher hot dog to me. Gee, Jerry, since my clubs were locked safely in the trunk of your Rolls, and you have the only key, I wonder who would have done such a thing?"

It was a big mystery all right. And good ol' Jerry, my buddy Jerry, was trying to help me get to the bottom of it all. Jerry quickly came to the conclusion that if it really was a kosher hot dog, then in all probability, the culprit was Jewish.

"But who do you know that's Jewish?" Jerry asked in a very mysterious voice.

"Let's see, who do I know that's Jewish?" I asked the question while fixing my eyes on Jerry's golf bag. Of course, just because Jerry had bold lettering on the side of his golf bag spelling out the name *Super Jew,* I didn't think he had anything to do with the great hot dog mystery. No, not Jerry.

"Oh," I told Jerry, "don't worry. Someday, I'll figure out who did it. And then, I'll get even."

Without cleaning the mustard off my driver, I began hitting balls. Pretty soon I was laughing. Then Jerry started laughing. Once Jerry got started, there was no stopping him. Before long Jerry was doing scenes from his movie, *The Caddy.* He really looked like a total klutz swinging the club. Jerry and I were just having some fun.

Then, out of the corner of my eye, I noticed a little guy standing near the tennis courts. Since he was wearing shorts, I figured he was probably a part of the tennis crowd at La Costa. But I couldn't be sure because he was sort of hiding behind the canvass surrounding the courts... sort of like peeking out from around the corner of the fence.

Suspicious of strangers, I started to keep an eye on the man. He was a skinny little guy with even skinnier legs. My God, I thought, paint them legs white and they'd make a couple of good OB markers on the golf course.

To tell you the truth, the little man didn't look threatening in any way. But all the same, he might be a deranged and wacky fan of Jerry's. One never knew what evil was lurking out there. Just to be safe I decided to keep and eye on the little guy.

But then, I looked at my driver and saw mustard smears. Suddenly I had another thought. Maybe I should excuse myself and hope the little guy was a deranged fan stalking Jerry. On second thought I better not because it was going to be more fun getting even on my own terms. And, I would get even.

Several minutes later the little man started walking toward us. "Jerry. Jerry Lewis," the little man said as he approached. "I thought that was you. I didn't realize you were such an accomplished golfer. What a beautiful swing."

Accomplished golfer? Beautiful swing? I asked myself the questions. Heck, Jerry was clowning around. He was hacking up. A complete klutz. Was the little guy blind?

Jerry turned, immediately recognized the man and said, "Hi Bobby."

The little man was Bobby Riggs, former tennis great.

Jerry introduced me and we spent several minutes chitchatting. Then Bobby started praising Jerry's swing.

"I was standing over by the tennis courts watching and wondering what touring pro was in town," Bobby sounded sincere. "Then I said, 'that's Jerry Lewis.' You sure have a sweet swing, Jerry."

Bobby Riggs wore glasses, but he wasn't blind. He had to know that Jerry was clowning around. That wasn't Jerry's swing. What was Bobby trying to do?

I had heard stories, probably nothing more than malicious rumors about Bobby Riggs hanging around La Costa "hustling" unsuspecting folks on the courts and links. But I never believed those stories about

Bobby hustling for a living. Naw, not Bobby.

Well, knock me over with a feather, but the next thing out of Bobby's mouth was something about playing Jerry for a little money. And Bobby, the sportsman that he was, suggested that he and Jerry play even. "Judging from your swing," Bobby said, "You're probably two or three shots better than me. But this is my home course, so we'll just play even. Okay?"

Now I'm not the brightest guy in the world, but if Bobby Riggs wanted to play Jerry even, that meant he felt he was about twenty shots better. Unbelievable, but Mr. Hustler actually thought Jerry was a klutz golfer.

I didn't know how good Bobby was, but I had played a lot of golf with Jerry. Surely someone was going to step forward and warn Bobby that he might be getting in over his head. Under normal conditions, I would have said something. But Jerry wasn't a big-time golf course gambler. Oh, sure we played for a few bucks every now and then, but golf was Jerry's way of getting out from under the daily grind of work. Golf was a way to have a little fun. I figured Jerry would say "no thanks" and that would be the end of it.

However, Bobby wouldn't take no for an answer. I understood. Any hustler worth his weight in salt would know that Jerry had a lot of money. And what's more, Bobby honestly believed Jerry was a hack. This could be the mother load.

Finally, Jerry got that look in his eyes and said, "Let's do it." This wasn't Jerry Lewis as *The Caddy*. This was Jerry Lewis going on a mission.

Several years earlier, I had seen the same look in Jerry's eyes. We had traveled to the islands for a Pro-Am, the Hawaiian – Northern California Open. After our practice round we were on the putting green when two jerks approached us. They were also in the tournament and they wanted a little action. You know, someone to pay for all of their traveling and lodging expense.

Jerry politely said, "No thanks."

We must have looked like a couple of easy pigeons because they really started running their mouths. They were obnoxious and even insulting.

Enough was enough. I said to Jerry, "Come on. They want some action, let's give 'em some action. We got enough daylight for just about nine holes."

When Jerry looked at me, I knew it was money in the bank. He had that look in his eyes, the totally focused look of a winner. He said, "Let's do it."

We did it. I shot even par 36 and tied the pro. But Jerry threw a neat little 33 at the amateur. There weren't too many amateurs in the world who would have beaten Jerry that day. When Jerry got that look in his eyes, it was like I said, money in the bank.

And so, here we were, Jerry, Bobby and me, standing on the first tee at La Costa. I thought it was kind of funny. Bobby was licking his chops thinking about the sacrificial lamb he had lured into the trap while Jerry just stood back with that look in his eyes. But with easy dollars signs flashing in Bobby's mind, he never took a real good look at his opponent. From my point of view, Jerry didn't look like a lamb about to be led to slaughter.

Slaughter was the word that kept bouncing around in my mind as Jerry and Bobby went at it. I don't remember exactly what Bobby and Jerry played for... maybe fifty dollars a hole, maybe a hundred. But I do remember Bobby won the same number of holes I did. But I wasn't playing. I was just watching. Heck, I would have paid to see this one, but Jerry let me come along for free.

After nine holes Bobby stammered, stuttered and then mumbled something about leaving his wallet in his other pants. And his other pants were in the locker room.

"I've got to get my wallet," Bobby explained. "But you wait, because I'll be right back."

Bobby turned the golf cart away from the tenth tee, put the pedal to the medal, and nearly burned a little rubber as he sped toward the club house. "Just wait there," he repeated. "because I'll be right back."

Yeah sure, I thought. He'd be right back just as soon as Jerry left town.

Bright and early the next morning we arrived at the course ready for the tournament. Since I was such a nice guy, I helped the caddies get Jerry's clubs out of the back of the Rolls. But, I insisted on personally carrying his brand new Footjoy shoes into the locker room. I didn't want Jerry to lose his brand new Footjoys.

Inside the locker room, Jerry sat down and put on a brand new pair of white, Wigwam socks. Jerry had this thing about wearing brand new, white, Wigwam socks every day.

Handing Jerry his new Footjoys, I sat back and watched as he slid his foot into the first shoe. Something was wrong. Jerry forced his foot a little and then realized something was stuck near the toe. Pulling his foot out of the shoe, I noticed some meat smashed on the sock.

"Gee, Jerry," I said. "That looks like salami and maybe a little bologna stuck to your brand new Wigwams. Now who the heck would put salami and bologna inside your new shoes?"

I've got to hand it to Jerry because the expression on his face never changed. He looked inside the shoe and began to remove enough salami and bologna for a couple of sandwiches.

Setting the first shoe down, he picked up the other one and asked, "Both shoes?"

"How would I know? Jerry... I hope you don't think I put salami and bologna in both of your brand new shoes."

Jerry looked into the toe of the second shoe. He almost smiled. Then he began removing the salami and bologna piece by piece, chunk by chunk. Jerry never said a word, but he knew it and so did I. I kept my promise. I got even with the Jewish guy who put the mustarded hot dog in my head cover.

I've mentioned the name Jerry had painted on his golf bag – *Super Jew*. There is no doubt in my mind, that in our politically correct, thin-skinned world, someone is going to be outraged by that name. But Jerry was Jewish and he was a super, super human being.

Over the years, things have really changed. I'm talking about the nonsense of political correctness. I remember a time, I think it was 1976, when Dean Martin was playing at Bally's Casino. He was on stage doing his routine when the audience went wild. The crowd started clapping, cheering, whistling and shouting. Dean turned to his left and saw Jerry standing there. They had gone their separate ways in 1956 and had only seen each other one time during those twenty years. But now, they hugged each other and began talking, reminiscing about the old days. Jerry and Dean talked about how much they missed each other. Both spoke of how sorry they were for going separate ways. Then Jerry asked Dean, "What happened? Why'd we split?"

And Dean Martin answered as only Dean Martin could, "Oh, I don't know. You called me a Jew and I called you a Dago."

Jerry quickly explained in his high pitched Jerry Lewis voice, "No, no. You're the Dago and I'm the Jew."

The audience fell out of their seats laughing. But in today's world, some folks would have run Dean and Jerry out of town for saying something like that. In this day and age we can't make jokes like that anymore. Forgive me, but I thought it was funny back then and I still think it's funny today. Jerry was Jewish and Dean was Italian. They made a little joke about it. Period.

Now there was a time when the name painted on Jerry's golf bag put us in a precarious situation. I'm talking about a very precarious situation

– life threatening and it happened in Greensboro, North Carolina during a golf tournament.

I was working at the Sahara when the call came. The Jaycees were sponsoring the Greenboro Open and they wanted Jerry for the Pro-Am. Since the tournament was about charity and golf, I was reasonably sure Jerry would want to attend.

This time, instead of receiving one of those "Jim, get your clubs and let's go," phone calls from Jerry in the middle of the night, I was about to return the favor. I stayed up later than normal. Then, I called Jerry hoping he would be in bed sleeping. But he wasn't. He was wide awake. When I mentioned golf, he was ready to go.

Jerry and I went to Greensboro a day early and met some wonderful people. Everything was first-class and we couldn't have been happier. We were having a terrific time. But then came tournament day.

Actually, the tournament started on a high note. State officials were there, local celebrities, national TV and a crowd of more than 30,000 spectators showed up because of Jerry. The tournament director said normal crowds for the Pro-Am usually topped off around eight thousand. But the Jaycees did a lot of promotional work and people came from all over the area to see Jerry. I heard someone say that Sam Snead was coming, too. They even said Sam was a big Jerry Lewis fan.

Our group, which included Jerry, myself, the Governor of North Carolina and the President of the Jaycees was scheduled to tee off last. By the time we got our ten minute call, the course was backed up and the tournament was a little behind schedule. So, Jerry and the Governor stood on the first tee talking quietly while I was off to the side taking a few practice swings. That's when it started. I heard someone in the crowd say, "Look at that $%&# golf bag of his. Look what the $%&# he gots writ on 'at bag."

"Gots writ on 'at bag?" I sort of repeated the statement in the form of

One of the greatest relationships of my life. Jerry is closer than a brother, more endearing than a friend. I love the guy!

a question. Now what the heck was that supposed to mean?

Oh, yeah, I thought while remembering what Jerry had on his bag – *Super Jew*.

Turning toward the gallery I saw trouble. There were a dozen or so of them standing in the middle of the crowd. They were some tough-looking characters. They wore heavy boots, dark clothes, and had more tattoos than a drunken Merchant Marine. Furthermore, every one of them had a bottle of beer in their hand. I had never seen tougher-looking girls in my life.

The guys were another story. They were real mean-looking. But I understood. Any normal, healthy guy would get a little mean after spending time with those... ah... gals?

The misfits were standing off to the side of the first tee and having what I can only describe as something of a tail-gate party. There was trash, beer and whiskey bottles scattered all over the ground. Sure an ugly girl will drive a man to drinking, but I didn't understand how these characters could get past the front gate in the first place. They were drunken trash. Slobs. Low lifers. Where was security?

A moment later, Jerry was introduced to the crowd. Just as he was ready to hit, one of rogues shouted, "I didn't know you %$#& Jews could play golf!"

Although Jerry kept going as though nothing were said, I could tell he was POed. He topped his first drive, but on the surface, Jerry pretended to be cool. As we got into the golf cart, Jerry made a little joke about the shot and we were off. Jerry drove and I rode shotgun. And believe me, this was one time I was wishing my fourteenth club was a shotgun. Maybe, I told myself, they'll go home and we can still have a nice day out on the course. But they didn't head for the exits. They started to follow our group.

We could hear the cat-calls, those verbal insults. Okay, I thought, we have some losers in the crowd, but where is security? Someone should run these characters off the course and out the front gate.

After several holes, enough was enough. I told Jerry, "Let's go. Let's get out of here."

"No," Jerry said. "We've got to stick it out. We just won't pay any attention to them and everything will be okay."

We didn't pay any attention to them. We pretended they weren't there. But it wasn't working. They continued launching bigoted remarks, and I kept mumbling to myself, "Sticks and stones will break my bones but names will never hurt me."

Then she stepped forward from the crowd and began walking toward the golf cart. Oh my, but this gal had the potential to really hurt someone. If she stumbled and fell on the golf cart Jerry and I would be crushed to death.

Wearing only tight-fitting jeans, a tube top, and with most of her drooping body parts exposed, the sight of this barnyard creature, puffing on a cigarette made my stomach turn. Then came the odor and suddenly I was nauseated. Wow! This beast needed to take a shower because anything that walked upright was not intended to smell like she smelled.

Then she leaned into the golf cart, looked me directly in the eye and demanded Jerry's autograph. I was staggered for a moment, nearly knocked down for the count. But even in my semi-conscious state, I knew that a toothbrush, toothpaste and strong mouthwash would never work on her Godzilla breath.

For the past several hours, this "woman" and her friends had been calling Jerry names. And now she wanted his autograph.

"Ma'am," I said while holding my breath, "we still have another hole to play. You'll have to wait until the tournament is over for an autograph."

She looked at me with a cocky smirk on her beefy face and said, "Wait my &%#$."

Immediately thereafter, I detected the smell of burning flesh. Then the pain, the excruciating pain registered. "HEY!" I screamed while pulling back my arm. The smell of burning flesh was my flesh burning. This thing... this creature had taken her cigarette and crushed it against my arm. Wow! That hurt!

This was supposed to be a golf tournament. But it had quickly deteriorated into an embarrassment for the sponsors and good people of Greensboro. It was unbelievable, but a few rogues had spoiled the day for everyone.

Once again, I could only wonder, where was security?

I attempted to push her back as Jerry hit the pedal on the golf cart. Fortunately, she was more of a waddler than a sprinter and we made good our escape. But Jerry insisted he wasn't going to let a few bigots ruin the day. He drove to the eighteenth tee and continued the round of golf.

Five or ten minutes later, with his ball plugged in a fairway bunker on the 18th hole, Jerry was considering whether to lay up or take a full swing and go for the green. The smart move was to get the ball back on the fairway and play for an up and down par. Taking a wedge, he decided to play it smart.

Jerry was preparing to hit the ball when we heard the guttural sounds. Looking toward the eighteenth tee, I saw her and her male companion approaching. Oh my God. With beer bottles in hand, both of them were making a lot of noise about the *autograph*. She still wanted her autograph.

At that particular time I felt there were more important things to do than finish the tournament. I simply didn't relish the thought of that gal leaning on the golf cart and crushing both of us. There were better ways to die.

I told Jerry, "Let's forget about golf and get out of here."

But Jerry wasn't going to let a couple of buttholes ruin his day. He stepped into the bunker, rushed the shot and bladed the ball. I had to admire Jerry's tenacity, but with the sunlight being blotted out by two foul mouths screaming about the autograph, I thought we'd be better served looking for an escape route.

The long and short of the story was that Jerry finished his round of golf. At least I think he finished, but I didn't. Instead, I was whacked in the head with a beer bottle and punched in the nose. Finally, security arrived.

Earl Nordtvedt, a friend of mine playing in the tournament, hid Jerry and me under the bleachers near the eighteenth green while the good folks from Burns Detective and other security people fought back the beast, her boyfriend and the rest of the gang. You see, by now, the rest of the hooligans were there. It was quite a battle.

Several minutes later someone said, "Here comes the limo."

With that, Jerry, Earl and I grabbed our clubs and ran for the limo. Once inside we locked the doors. We were safe... or so I thought.

At the exact moment I thought we were on the high ground, some guy started pounding on the side of the limo. And Earl, for whatever the reason, pressed the button and lowered the window. Evidently it wasn't over. We weren't safe because a guy wearing a straw hat was trying to climb in through the window while shouting "Jerry! Jerry!"

I took a swing at the guy, knocked his cheap straw hat off as Jerry tried to shove him out of the limo. This guy was tough! He really wanted to get Jerry!

"Let's go!" I told the driver as I pushed the button and the window slid up nearly choking the guy. He was lucky, because I really wanted to get that window up around his neck and drag him all the way to the airport. And believe me, the airport was where we were going.

Speeding away from the clubhouse, I looked out the back window and saw the guy getting up. As he stood there brushing the dirt from his clothes, I couldn't help but think there was something familiar about him.

Then I turned and noticed his hat was still in the back seat of the limo. Darn, there was something familiar about the hat. I lowered the window, flung the hat out and said, "No one will be able to get us now. We're safe."

The driver of the limo glanced in his rearview mirror and casually explained the facts. "I don't think you understand, but that guy wasn't trying to get Mr. Lewis or anyone. He just wanted to say hello. That was Sam Snead."

Hopefully someone would tell Sam the entire story because we weren't going back to explain or apologize. We were going to the airport and climbing aboard the next flight west.

While flying toward the setting sun, Jerry and I didn't say much to each other. There wasn't much we could say. It was a bad day, a real bad day, and I had a burn on my arm, a bump on my head and a broken nose to prove it. Sure my injuries hurt, but Jerry was hurting even more. This should have been a good day, a fun time. It wasn't. Jerry didn't deserve to be subjected to any of this. No one did.

As I nursed my wounds, I began to think about Jerry. It was a collection of thoughts, random thoughts that passed before me like a motion picture. I remembered the times when he made people laugh. And I could never forget the many times his friendship and generosity brought tears to my eyes. Then I thought about the many occasions when he gave of himself and his time and his money to charities. And of course, I thought about his telethon for Muscular Dystrophy and the millions of research dollars he had raised so that medical science could help those little children. No, Jerry didn't deserve any of this. No one did.

I watched as Jerry drifted off to sleep. "Jerry Lewis," I whispered, "I really got us into a bad one today." But then I smiled because I knew what tomorrow would bring. By tomorrow everything would get back to normal. Tomorrow would present Jerry with more opportunities to make people laugh, more golf tournaments, more charities to help, more planning for his next telethon or perhaps work on a Broadway production or a new movie.

And as for me? Well... with things getting back to normal I was positive there would be more of those early morning phone calls from that familiar voice checking to be sure I was awake, wide awake, and then the dial tone. Jerry claimed he was an early riser but I maintain he was and still is more of a late night practical joker.

But no matter how late or early the phone would ring, I always answered knowing it was going to be Jerry. And, of course, once he established the fact he had roused me from a deep sleep, he'd hang up.

Yeah, Jerry would get me, but I really didn't care. You see, we were both guilty of playing practical jokes on each other. But the real test of our relationship came when one of us would make the phone call and say, "Get your clubs and let's go." And in those magical adventures born of golf clubs and golf balls, both good and bad, I came to realize that I had a friend... and a wonderful and true friend at that. But isn't that what the good life is all about, having family and a few good friends?

Art Gatts, his wife, Jerry's wife Patty, yours truly, Earl Nordtvedt and Jerry, my team at the Hawaiian Pro-Am.

I have many terrific memories of Dean Martin, especially on the course. He loved the game as much as anyone I have seen. He was a funny guy, a good golfer and believe it or not, off stage, Dean was very quiet, almost shy. However this picture is how I will always remember Dean Martin.

8

Everybody Loves Somebody Sometime

It was a small gathering of Jerry's friends, my wife and me along with his manager, Joe Stabile, and Joe's wife, Claudia. We were sitting in the green room at the Space Center of the Sahara Hotel watching the Jerry Lewis Muscular Dystrophy Telethon.

Actually, I had the best seat in the house. I was sitting in front of the television, but if I turned my head to the right, I could look out of the room and through the slightly parted curtain and see Jerry preforming live on stage. During the telethon, Jerry always liked to have several of his friends sitting nearby. So, when Jerry called and said he wanted me to be there, I dropped everything and got on the plane. If Jerry felt that my being there would help him, then I wanted to be there for the duration. And I do mean duration. The telethon went on for twenty-four hours, and Jerry, with little or no sleep, stayed with it for that period of time. Jerry's energy level was incredible. Mine wasn't and after twelve or thirteen hours, I was getting a little tired.

Jerry was well into the telethon when the commotion began outside of the green room. I heard a reluctant voice say, "I'm not going to do it."

Then a second voice said, "If you don't do it, I'm gonna have the boys break your &#$% legs."

Suddenly, two very large men entered the green room and glared at everyone. "All right," the biggest of the two men said, "I want youse to get the #&$% outta here."

I didn't know who this "youse" person was, but if I was he, I would have gotten out of the room immediately. The gentleman telling Mr. Youse to leave was big. Really big.

Once again, from outside, I heard the same voice say, "I'm not going to do it!"

And once again I heard, "I'm telling you, if you don't do it, I'm gonna have the boys break your &$%# legs."

"Now go on," the largest man said, "all of youse get the &$%# outta here!"

For some reason, I was beginning to think "all of youse" meant all of us. Joe Stabile must have gotten the same impression because he stood up and said, "I'm Jerry's manager. Is there something I can help you with?"

"Yeah," the large man said, "just get the &$%# outta here. All of youse."

I was positive that Joe was staying and if he was staying, I would stay, too. In other words, we weren't going to let Bruno, or whatever his name was, chase us. Just as I was about to stand up, the Chairman of The Board himself entered the room, Frank Sinatra. And following behind Frank was Dean Martin.

Now I should explain that the "boys," two of them that is, had Dean by the arms and were actually dragging him into the room. And just for the record, Dean made it quite clear that he wouldn't do whatever Frank wanted him to do. And again, and for the record, Frank made it extremely clear that if Dean didn't do what he wanted him to do, then the boys were going to break Dean's legs.

Suddenly, I wasn't tired. I was wide awake and all eyes. This had the potential to become a very interesting night.

Dean glanced up and saw me. He seemed surprised. And so typical of the fun-loving guy that he was, he asked, "Hey, Jimbo, what are you doing here?"

I had known Dean for several years and had played a lot of golf with him in Los Angeles. He was always a fun guy to be around. But tonight, if he was surprised to see me, I was shocked to see him... to see him under these conditions that is.

"Gee, Dean, I guess the better question would be, what are you doing here?" I asked.

"Getting my legs broken if I don't go out on the stage and say hello to what's his name," Dean answered as only Dean could.

"And that's right," Frank warned. "If you don't go out on that stage and get together with him, so help me, I'll have the boys break your &$%# legs."

Dean started making a lot of noise, so the "boys" took him out of the green room and locked him in one of the production trailers. Then Frank explained to Joe Stabile that the "boys" had kidnaped Dean in Los Angeles, sobered him up and flew him to Las Vegas on a private plane for a reunion with Jerry.

At the time, Dean and Jerry hadn't talked to each other for years. "But tonight," Frank promised, "he can walk out on the stage with two good legs and make up with Jerry, or the boys will drag him out with broken legs. Either way, he is going on stage and he's going to make up with Jerry."

I thought, broken legs or not, it would be a momentous occasion – Martin and Lewis together again. Everyone in the world knew their story, how they accidently formed an act and became overnight sensations. And then, ten years to the day, they went different ways and never spoke to each other again. What a surprise this would be for the world. What a surprise for Jerry.

During the time I spent with Jerry, I never asked him about Dean. I never asked the obvious question. What went wrong? And Jerry never mentioned Dean Martin. Not one time. Not ever.

It was the same way with Dean. There were times when Dean and I would golf, then race cross town in his sports car to the studios in Burbank for his show, *The Gold Diggers,* and go out afterwards until the wee hours of the early morning. And during those times, Dean would get nostalgic. He'd talk about growing up in Steubenville, Ohio. "It was a tough town, Jimbo, a river town that had fallen on hard times. I tried boxing, working in a steel mill, card sharking and then singing. I worked the bars and local clubs around the area. Finally, I came to New York. I was scratching out a living... then I went to Atlantic City for a few days and got lucky... really lucky."

With the mention of Atlantic City, I knew what Dean meant. That was where he and Jerry got started. But the conversation never went any further. I never, not once, ever heard Dean Martin mention the name Jerry Lewis. Dean would talk about his wife, his kids, how much he loved them, but those chapters of life which concerned Jerry Lewis never came up. And interestingly enough, I always had the feeling that Dean Martin still loved Jerry very much. And the same held true for Jerry in that he still loved Dean.

Dean Martin was one of the most mellow individuals I had ever met. I never saw him get mad, and I never heard him say an unkind word about anyone. And believe me, he had reason to go off on some of his friends.

The story that sticks in my mind is how Dean's alleged friends would wait for him to come to the golf course. Everyone would be standing around, licking their chops, waiting for Dean. Of course, this friendship was based on Dean's ability to pay off his bets. What I mean to say is that these so-called friends of Dean would get him in an unfair bet, beat him and collect. I never saw Dean win a golf match and I never heard Dean complain about losing to his friends.

One day, instead of playing with his friends, it was just Dean and I. And right away, on the first tee he said, "Let's have a little action, Jimbo. How about one hundred dollars three ways?"

I told Dean I didn't play for that kind of money. He shrugged his shoulders and said, "Okay, make it twenty bucks three ways."

"That sounds closer to my budget," I said. "How many strokes do you want?"

"Strokes!" Dean raised his voice. "I'll play you even."

"Dean, I'm a pro... scratch... you're not," I tried to reason with Dean.

"But, you don't understand, Jimbo. I don't mind losing."

We played, but we didn't play even. I was a pro, and Dean was an amateur shooting in the high seventies to the low eighties. I gave him five a side, and beat him three ways. Afterwards, I mentioned something to the effect that I felt his golfing friends took advantage of him. "They're not interested in a fair bet, Dean. They're interested in fleecing you."

Dean smiled and said, "I know that Jimbo. I know they sit and wait for me to show up. I know they think they're sucking me in. But I don't mind losing. After all, it's only money."

Kind, generous and easygoing is the only way to describe Dean. And truthfully, Jerry was the same way. Sure, during the days of their partnership, Dean was the man with a song who ended up with the women, and Jerry was the clown. But in real life they were very much the same – kind, generous and easygoing. I wonder what went wrong?

My thoughts about Martin and Lewis were interrupted when I heard Frank Sinatra tell one of the boys, "Okay, it's time. Go on and get him. And, let him know, he can walk out on stage with healthy legs or we'll slide him out with broken ones. Either way is fine with me because one way or another he's going out there and make up with Jerry."

To my surprise, Dean wasn't combative. I guess I could say that while Dean was locked up in the trailer, he sort of had an attitude adjustment. He was really mellowed out and ready to see Jerry.

Now, I'm not inferring that one of the "boys" went into the trailer and beat up Dean, because that would be the furthest thing from the truth. Dean's attitude adjustment was solely the result of whose trailer he had been confined to.

When I saw Dean enter the green room, I suddenly remembered Frank telling the story about the boys kidnapping and sobering him up. Frank even went as far as to say they hid all the booze on the plane so that Dean would pass a sobriety test for the historical meeting with Jerry. But, unfortunately or maybe fortunately, the trailer Dean was locked in for the past hour belonged to Ed MacMahon.

For those of you who do not understand the implication, let's just say that Ed MacMahon was reputed to enjoy an adult beverage every now and then. And, obvious to everyone who watched as Dean wobbled into the room, Ed's trailer was now no doubt bone dry.

I stood back and watched as Frank parted the curtain, and on wobbling but not broken legs, Dean Martin walked out on stage for his reunion with Jerry.

Sitting here years later, I think about that night, and often I wonder what happened to Martin and Lewis, what went wrong? But now, it's too late to ask Dean and I've never asked Jerry.

As I mentioned previously, Jerry and Dean got together for a second time after their forced meeting at the Space Center. Dean was playing in Vegas when all of a sudden the audience started shouting and applauding. Dean turned to his left and saw Jerry standing there. They hugged and Jerry asked, "What happened to us?"

Dean answered, "Oh, I don't know... I called you a Dago and you called me a Jew."

"No, no," Jerry said. "I'm the Jew and you're the Dago."

Then, in unison they said, "I love you." They hugged each other and the audience stood as the building shook with a thunderous ovation. Once again, it was Martin and Lewis.

The comedy act of the century, Martin and Lewis in their prime.

Rodeos are big in Reno and when the cowboys came to town, I let them know I was a cowboy, too. I don't know why they always laughed at me.

9

Why He Should Quit Golfing

There was a time when I thought I had seen and heard it all... all about golf that is. I've seen the good guys and the bad guys of the game and I've heard sad stories and funny stories. In fact, the pages of this book are filled with good stories, funny stories, stories to warm a person's heart. It's like I said, there was a time when I thought I had seen and heard it all – the good, the bad and the ugly of the game.

Take, for example, Gary Player. Most folks think Gary is a real straight shooter with an impeccable reputation. Not true. I'm here to tell you that every time Gary tees off, there are whispers to "keep an eye on him." It was so bad for Gary on tour that his playing partners would keep an eye on him and their caddies would watch his caddie, Alfred "Rabbit" Dyer.

A number of years ago, there was an article in the *San Francisco Sunday Examiner & Chronicle* by Mark Soltau which detailed some of Gary's and Rabbit's on-course, alleged, nefarious activities.

Soltau wrote about the British Open when Gary hit a wild tee shot beyond the crowd and into the bushes. As the specators were trying to show Gary where the ball landed, Rabbit found a ball, Gary's ball in the rough near the edge of the fairway. At least Rabbit identified the ball as Gary's.

Needless to say, the spectators were baffled. After all, they saw Gary's ball fly into the brush and yet Rabbit found the ball forty or fifty yards away. Naturally, Gary played the ball Rabbit found and naturally an unconvinced spectator went into the brush and found a ball, a ball the spectator was positive belonged to Gary.

Granted, I wasn't there so I couldn't attest to validity of that particular Gary Player story either way. However, I do know that Johnny Miller and his former caddie, Andy Martinez, along with Tom Watson, are not avid fans of Gary's. In fact, they are on record as questioning some of Gary's tactics. Especially the favorable lies he usually seems to find in the roughs. But again, since I wasn't there to see it for myself, the matter is nothing more than one man's word against another.

But there was that one time when I did tee it up with Gary, and I know what my eyes saw. This eventful day happened in the early 1960s at the Utah Open. Gary Player was scheduled to play, but he was running late. He should have been disqualified but this was, of course, Gary Player. Instead of DQing Gary, the director held up the tournament. Finally, the little man arrived.

Since Gary was late, all the lockers had been assigned. But what the heck. I had one of the more spacious lockers, so I offered to share mine with Gary. Instead of a quiet thank you from the visiting South African, he made a gutteral sound and said, "I don't share a locker with anyone." Gary Player was arrogance personified.

I am really not a violent man. However, I did have the urge to shove my fist so far down Gary's throat that he would need a proctologist to remove it. But, we had a tournament to play and lucky me... Gary was in my grouping.

On the second or third hole, Gary started warming up to me. I hit a shot and Gary finally spoke. "What iron did you hit there?" he asked.

I never told Gary what club I had hit. In fact I never said a word. After all, I was a club pro and he was a touring pro. Gary had to know he had just broken a rule of golf. It's highly illegal to ask an opponent that question.

Then, on the forth hole, Gary hit his ball into the rough. The ball was sitting down. I was only about ten yards away from Gary, but I could tell he had a real tough lie. As he was fiddling around looking at the lie and checking distance, I turned and watched our other partner, Dick Kramer hit his shot.

A few second later, when I turned back toward Gary, I saw his ball was now setting up perfectly. He improved his lie and that is illegal.

It was a miserable day, trying to compete in a tournament while my insides were burning with anger. When we walked off the eighteenth green, I immediately went to the tournament officials and told them the story. I saw Gary improve a lie on two occasions and he asked me what club I hit three or four times. The tournament officials said that they didn't think Gary Player would do such a thing, and posted his score anyway. But I refused to sign his scorecard.

Yeah... I thought I had seen and heard it all... all about golf, that is. Why, I've seen Chi Chi Rodriguez and Lee Trevino treat fans like gold when the television cameras were on. But when the TV crew packed it up, Chi Chi and Lee would chase people away. And I've seen Arnold talk to his army and sign hundreds of autographs without even checking if there was a television camera nearby. Arnold is a real Prince, a King.

Hey, I understand how the fans can be and I know it works both ways. Several years ago at the Olympic Club in San Francisco, Greg Norman was practicing on the putting green just before he was scheduled to tee off. A fan walked up to Greg and asked him to autograph the program. Greg said, "I can't do it right now because I'm getting ready to tee off. See me afterwards."

Greg wasn't trying to be a wise guy. He was focusing his attention on the first tee, but at the same time he was very polite. But the fan took the progam and slapped Greg across the face with it.

Yeah, it's like I said, there was a time when I thought I had heard and seen it all... all about golf that is. But then, I had to make a trip to San

Diego for a visit to the Taylor Made Golf factory. I'm on the Taylor Made staff, and from time to time, I stop in at the PGA department to check out new equipment.

However, Bill Kushner, the fellow who helped out with my book (the words are mine, the periods and commas are Bill's), lives in San Diego. And from Bill's simple little suggestion about playing some golf while I was there, I would come to realize that I hadn't seen or heard it all.

After my visit to Taylor Made, Bill and I were off to Temeku Hills Golf Club, north of San Diego. Two of Bill's friends would join us for the round of golf, a fellow by the name of Dwight Dyck and another guy called "Pruner."

Pruner? I thought. No doubt it was a nickname, but a strange name at that. For some reason I got the feeling that Pruner was an older man, perhaps a man who needed a few prunes to get everything moving in the morning. But I would soon discover that Pruner was in his late forties and his name had more to do with trees than prunes.

Bill said, "The fact of the matter is Pruner can't play a round of golf without knocking branches off the trees, so many branches that he's affectionately known as The Pruner. Most people don't even know his real name. Come to think of it, I'm not sure he has a real name."

Before the day was over, I would not only see for myself that Pruner was more adept at pruning trees with a golf ball than hitting greens in regulation, but I would also arrive at the conclusion that perhaps he was, as Bill had said, "one of the world's worst avid golfers." But I am getting ahead of the story, so let me backtrack a little and tell it from start to finish.

As we drove into the parking lot at Temeku, Bill pointed and said "There's Dwight."

I really don't know how to describe what I saw. You see, the car door was opened and Dwight was sitting sideways. It looked as though he was changing shoes. But something was wrong, seriously wrong.

At first I thought I saw Dwight's legs dangling out of the car. Then I realized it wasn't legs. It was singular as in leg. One of Dwight's legs was normal. The ankle bone was connected to the knee bone and the knee bone was connected to the hip. But WOW the other leg had been wacked off above the knee, and it all must have happened recently.

Dwight was holding a foot... I mean he had a leg in his hand. At least it looked that way – his shoe was still on, but the leg wasn't. And then the blood. My God, there was blood everywhere. It looked like a massacre, a bloody massacre. Did someone side swipe Dwight's car and knock his leg off? How did this happen?

For having just arrived at the scene of such a bloody accident, Bill was rather casual. And so was Dwight. Bill rolled down his window and said to Dwight, "It looks good, real good. But make sure you bleed on the black top. I want Pruner to see blood all over the black top."

"Bleed on the black top?" I whispered to myself. I was sick to my stomach and Bill was telling Dwight that his bloodied stump looked good. Furthermore, he wanted Dwight to bleed on the black top.

The color drained from my face and I started searching out a place to heave. But then, Bill looked at me and said, "Hey, Jim... take it easy. It's not what you think. We're playing a little joke on Pruner."

I think Dwight realized I was getting sick. He held up his "leg" and said, "It's called a prosthetic device. It replaces the leg I lost several years ago. Don't worry, I didn't get my leg knocked off today. It's Bill's idea of a practical joke... a sick one, but a practical joke nonetheless."

I learned the practical joke actually began to take shape several weeks ago when Bill played a round of golf with Pruner at the home of the Shark Shoot Out, Sherwood Lakes Country Club. Bill told me that Pruner had a terrible day. "Jim, on the back nine alone, he went seventeen over on the par fives. He hit homes, launched one into the clubhouse, knocked branches off trees, got the caddie twice, hit one half way up MASH Mountain, and lost a dozen balls or so. The only green he hit in regulation was the eighteenth, but unfortunately we were playing the ninth hole at the time. The caddie said that Pruner was far and away the worst player to ever challenge Sherwood Lakes. And what does Pruner say after the round is over? He attempts to blame it all on his eye. He tells us that his eye was hurting. He had been hit in the eye with a baseball the night before and had a little bitty black eye."

I still didn't completly understand what was going on. How did a round of golf at Sherwood relate to what looked like a bloody massacre in the parking lot at Temeku?

Finally, Dwight said, "It's not real blood. It's theatrical blood. You see, I lost my leg in an auto accident two years ago. But Bill wanted me to meet his friend, Pruner, and he thought this would be a good way to get started."

Bill explained that after the Sherwood exibition, he accused Pruner of being a pantywaist, a real sissy. "Hey," Bill said, "being the world's worst avid golfer was one thing, but being a pantywaist was inexcusable. A little black eye. C'mon. So, I told Pruner I could go out and find someone with a real handicap... someone that didn't have an eye, or maybe someone that had lost and arm or a leg, and that person could come in here cold turkey and beat Pruner. And Dwight, the sport that he is, volunteered. Now the interesting thing about all this is the fact that Dwight carries and plays to a nine handicap and Pruner has the potential to go nine over par on every hole. It's a match Pruner can't win."

As it turned out Bill and Dwight were good friends. But Pruner had never met Dwight. "So," Dwight said as he poured a little theatrical blood over his stump and onto the black top, "Bill thought it would make for a great practical joke if we told Pruner I had my leg wacked off a couple of days ago, and sneaked out of the hospital for a little golf today."

This was of course a sick practical joke. However, it did have potential, but there was one problem. Would this Pruner guy fall for something like this? After all, getting a leg amputated was serious business... it's not exactly the type of surgery a guy has one day and is out on the course golfing the next.

I had to ask the obvious question. "Will this Pruner guy fall for it?"

Bill explained that Pruner was a civil engineer. "In other words," Bill said, "Pruner never sees the entire picture. He'll throw reason and logic out the window and focus on Dwight's missing leg and all the blood. Of course he'll fall for it."

With that said, Bill continued to make his case. He told me the story about a round of golf that he and Pruner had played at Carmel Mountain Ranch in San Diego with head pro Mike Winn and assistant, Jeff Vance. On that particular day, Jeff Vance switched putters with Pruner. Jeff and Pruner had the same putters, but there was a little difference. Jeff was right-handed and Pruner was left-handed. And oh yeah, Bill did mention that Jeff had white tape over the grip of his putter and Pruner didn't.

Dwight Dyck, Kermit Kerner, The Pruner and Bill Kushner.

"We watched," Bill said, "as Pruner lined up his putt with Jeff's putter in hand. Finally he stood over the ball and prepared to putt. But... something was wrong. It took Pruner a little while, but then he figured it out. Yeah, he figured it out... his putter head was on backwards and someone taped his grip."

So there you have it, the stage was set and all we had to do was wait for Pruner.

Five, maybe ten minutes later, Pruner arrived. As he pulled into the parking lot, Dwight began his routine of straping the prosthetic device to his bloodied stump. Pruner's reaction to the sight was no different than mine. He also looked a little sick.

Bill casually introduced Dwight and me to Pruner. Then he asked Pruner, "Do you remember what I told you at Sherwood... about getting someone with a real handicap and bringing that person out to give you a whipping?"

I wanted to laugh but I didn't because this show had the potential to become a classic. Pruner was going for it hook, line and sinker. And Dwight, not one to shy away from the spotlight told Pruner the story of how he had just lost his leg the other day, and that he felt a little woozy from the medication.

As Dwight stood and attempted to walk, Bill asked, "Does it hurt?"

"Naw," Dwight said. "But it does feel funny, all the blood sloshing around inside the prosthetic device."

Bill turned to me and said, "Jim, you're the pro here. Now if Dwight beats Pruner under these conditions, wouldn't you say that's more than enough of a reason as to why he should quit golfing?" Pruner was a real nice guy, but this was just too good of a joke to let him off the hook. "Well," I said, "under these conditions, I can't imagine Dwight being able to beat anyone. So, all I can say is I sure hope Pruner doesn't get beat today."

That night, after everything was over, I went back to my hotel room, laid down on the bed and thought about my encounter with Dwight and Pruner. Of course, Dwight won. He shot a 79 even though the blood was sloshing around inside of his prosthetic device and the medication had him seeing three balls at one time.

And as for Pruner, I can honestly say I have never seen a game quite like his. He had a birdie, five pars, a bogey, and eleven holes that we refer to as "others." But Pruner's golf course woes had little or nothing to do with a swing. His grip was a little strong, but the swing was solid. Pruner's major problem was trees. His golf balls seemed to gravitate toward the trees. Why, he spent so much time in the trees that he set the mating habits of the squirrels and birds back several months.

Now I'm not saying Pruner hit a tree with every shot because he didn't. He had a few errant shots which found other targets. He hit two homes, nailed a car going down a nearby road, and thinned a shot that killed a couple of coots at the water hole. According to Bill, Pruner had a typical day out on the course, "nothing out of the ordinary, just a typical run-of-the-mill day for Pruner."

Pruner might have lost his match with Dwight, but he isn't the world's worst avid golfer. He's far from it. He just has trouble with trees. Trees are always getting in the way of his golf balls. Heck, Pruner might go to Saudi Arabia some day, play a course without trees and become the Tiger Woods of the desert. However, until that happens, Pruner will have to put up with trees, practical jokes and a one-legged guy with a single digit handicap. But in spite of it all, my advice to Pruner is "keep swinging" because he has discovered the very essence of golf. And that is to enjoy the game and have fun. You see, that is the amazing and wonderful thing about the game of golf, all of us do not have to be scratch golfers in order to enjoy the sport. Anyone can pick up the sticks, go out on the course and have fun.

But, one word of caution to any and all southern California golfers – stay out of the woods if Pruner is playing the same course.

Keep swinging and have fun.

10

The Great Secret
To A Better Game

One day, while giving Dean Martin a few pointers on the chip shot, he suggested, "Jimbo, you should write a book on your teaching techniques. You have a way of keeping everything simple. You make it fun and... well... I'm a better golfer because of your unique style."

I was flattered to think that my approach to the game had helped Dean. But I had to let him know a book like that just wasn't a good idea. "To be honest," I said, "something like that just wouldn't work, Dean. You see, I don't believe a person can learn the game of golf by reading an instructional book."

"Well, if you can't do it with words, then do it with pictures. Put a lot of pictures in the book, and I'll buy one." Dean replied.

The truth of the matter is that to play the game of golf you must understand that you cannot find a golf game in a book. It's absolutely impossible to read through a golf instructional book and head for your golf course, tee it up and be mistaken for Tom Watson, Fred Couples, or any other golfer that plays the game of golf for a living.

Does anyone believe they can read a thesis on playing a musical instrument and then play with an orchestra? Does anyone think if they read a book about baseball, they'll be in the line-up with the Giants? Yeah, sure.

No teaching style or philosophy can be translated onto pages of text. The same holds true for a picture of the golf swing. Oh, sure, we can come to have a general understanding of the mechanics of the game by reading a book or looking at a picture, but there is no substitute for lessons under the watchful eye of a good PGA Pro and practice time at the range. Reading a book and looking at pictures simply creates too many swing thoughts whereas a good PGA Pro and practice time helps to create muscle memory.

Throughout my 45 years as a golf professional, I have never given two lessons alike.

I firmly believe that recreational players who can't break ninety do not understand the correct basic fundamentals. If you really want to improve your game... See a compotent PGA Professional!

I do find it rather interesting just how many golf instructional books are published every year. Furthermore there doesn't seem to be much of a shortage on published articles that can teach us all how to hit the ball as far as John Daly or putt like Ben Crenshaw. Does anyone really believe they will hit the ball like John Daly by reading an article in the monthly golf magazine? Evidently a lot of people do because someone keeps writing those type of golf tips and the magazines continually sell.

I believe most of the instructional golf books on the market and golf magazines with those colorful features do nothing more than confuse the average golfer. Aside from the basics, books and magazine articles alike have a tendency to contradict teaching styles or tips. Short back swing! Longer back swing! Pick the ball clean! Hit down on the ball! More hip and leg action! Quiet the hips and legs! Cluttering a person's mind with too many swing thoughts only serves to confuse.

I've even seen instructional books that contain a whole section on marking the ball. Marking the ball properly or improperly isn't going to make anyone a better golfer. We all know how to mark a ball properly, right?

Marking the ball

Place coin behind the ball, then lift the ball.

Remarking the ball

Place the ball in front of the coin and lift coin.

I'm not trying to be funny with this little illustration. It's just that I've played golf with people all over the world and not everyone knows how to mark a ball. I'm sure we've seen some of our playing partners fudge a little when remarking the ball. They might have a twenty-five foot putt.

But what do they do? They remark the ball several inches in front of the coin. Okay, now instead of a twenty five foot putt, they now have a 24 foot, 9 inch putt.

Just the mention of marking a ball, I'm reminded of an Asian man I golfed with several years ago. He spoke very little English and I knew virtually no Chinese. But we had the universal language of golf as a wonderful form of communication.

On the first hole, I marked my ball with a quarter. At least I thought I marked my ball with a quarter. But when my turn came to putt, I couldn't find my marker... my quarter.

I was looking for my quarter and my girlfriend, Diane was looking too. But it wasn't there. Unbelievable, I thought, I must be getting old. Even though I could swear I remembered marking my ball, I must have picked up my ball without marking it. Shame on me.

On the second hole, I marked my ball with a dime. But when my turn came to putt, I couldn't find my dime. This time I didn't say anything to Diane because I didn't want her to worry about the senile old man she was golfing with. I simply told myself after the round of golf was over, I'd call my doctor and have him check me out. Hey, I was concerned. I didn't like the prospects of seeing a stranger every time I looked in the mirror.

Then, several holes later, I breathed a sigh of relief. After my pocket change had been reduced to marking my ball with pennies, Diane came up to me and whispered, "I think that little man has been picking up your coins. I just saw him take your penny."

A diversion I know, but that is what books are supposed to be about – stories, and not words and pictures about the golf swing. At any rate, let me get back to the business at hand. And speaking of hand, let me begin with The Proper Grip.

Hold the club below the pad of your left hand and more with your fingers.

Place your thumb slightly right of the shaft.

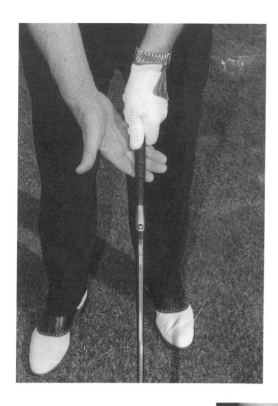

Hold fingers of right hand on the club as shown.

Place hands on the club with minimum pressure.

Okay, we have a clean, white glove and 4 steps to a proper grip. We can hold the club the proper way, but that doesn't mean we can swing it.

Next, we'll cover The Chip Shot.

The Chip Shot is a low shot that carries less than 1/3 of the way in the air, then rolls to the cup. This is the reason for his hands being in front of the clubhead at impact.

Note that the hands stay in front of the clubhead through the shot.

Okay, a photograph and a few words can give a person the basics of chipping the proper way. But we still need to see our PGA Pro in order to refine the technique and of course, practice helps, too.

Quick & Easy Tip

On the range, always practice with a purpose.
Just beating on balls is useless.

Beyond Parallel

This is Diane, my girlfriend and we are trying to illustrate a bad position at the top of the swing. Notice the clubhead has traveled beyond parallel. Unless you're John Daly, you don't want to start the forward swing from this position.

The Proper Position

This is a photograph of perfect club position at the top of the back swing.

The Perfect Swing

The next six photographs are stop action of the perfect golf swing. Of course, the little girl is not only a student of mine, but my 13-year old granddaughter, Katie Federici.

Figure 1: Focus on the shoulder turn. Observe her steady head throughout the swing... an absolute must.

Figure #2: Retain angle between shaft of club and left arm.

Figure #3: Notice the straight line from left shoulder to club head.

Figure #4: Head stays down and behind the ball.

Figure #5: Balance - weight on the left side.

Figure #6: Finish high.

The point in all of this is that most of us will never swing like Fred Couples or Davis Love III or Tiger Woods no matter how many golf books and magazines we read or pictures we see. But at the same time, we are all unique in our own way, blessed with our own special talents. However, in order to maximize those talents as they relate to golf, it begins with a qualified PGA Pro and practice time at the range. Sure we can learn the basics from a book and perhaps come to understanding the swing a little better by looking at a picture, but the great secret to a better game is your local pro.

For a better game, see your local pro like these students of mine did.

> ## Quick & Easy Tip
>
> ## THIN IRON SHOTS:
> *Instead of focusing on the ball,*
> *look at a blade of grass directly under the ball.*

Working with my buddy, Vic Damone at Pebble Beach.

> ## Quick & Easy Tip
>
> ### During a round of golf, keep your mind on what is important – The next shot only. TOO MUCH ANALYSIS, CREATES PARALYSIS!

Working with a student of mine, Rocky Lepori on some of the finer points of the golf swing.

And on the subject of the local pro, I will say this. If your pro comes out to give you a lesson with a glove on and clubs in hand, beware. Remember, it's your lesson and you should be the one hitting the golf balls.

I remember one time I watched as a local pro prepared to give a fellow a lesson. He came out to the range with his shoes on and packing his bag. But... wait a second here... that's another story, a story I just might put in my next golfing book.

Quick & Easy Tip

Most Importantly...
RELAX AND ENJOY THIS GREAT GAME!

One extra tip for all you avid golfers, there's more to life than golf. As a golf professional, the game has been a big part of me, but I have always remembered to enjoy the finer things in life... family, friends and fun.

It's me and my girlfriend, Diane Heltzel. One heck of a golfer, lady and friend. Here we are, still smiling after 12 years together and over 8,000 holes of golf.

INDEX

About the Authors

JIM CHENOWETH

Jim began his professional athletic career as a baseball player for the New York Giants organization in the late 1940's as a pitcher. After he suffered a serious injury that ended baseball as a profession, he began succeeding in the game of golf. Jim started the tour and won many tournaments and opens throughout the 1950's and 1960's. Jim soon discovered his teaching talents were in high demand and decided to devote his entire golfing career to helping others achieve excellence in their game.

Jim is known throughout the United States as the "Pro's Pro." He has instructed many touring professionals such as Tom Shaw, Bob Lunn, Rod Curl, as well as numerous others, including amateur champions. Jim has taught such celebrities as the legendary Bing Crosby, Jerry Lewis, Milton Berle, Pat Boone, Clint Eastwood and others.

Honored on the Mike Douglas Super Star Show as America's top teaching professional for golf, professionals all over the country know they can depend on Jim for assistance with any problem they may have from tee to green. Jim has originated many golf schools, has been chosen Director of Golf for the Del Webb resort and Bally's Casino Resort in Reno, Nevada.

Jim hosted his own syndicated television show, "Swinging With The Stars" in the late 1970's. He has designed golf courses all over the state of Nevada and Northern California. Most recently, Mr. Chenoweth was featured as one of America's top golf professionals in Japan's Golf Digest with over 8 million readers.

Jim Currently tours the nation promoting his new book *From Tee*

To Green To Hollywood, his innovative audio tape, *Mind Over Golf*, revolutionary video tape *Video School of Golf*, putting on clinics, appearing at tournaments, providing instruction to his students as well as being the president of his own golf services company, Jim Chenoweth Enterprises.

BILL KUSHNER

Bill Kushner was born in Sharon, Pennsylvania, and grew up in Brookfield, Ohio. After a brief stint with the New York Jets, Bill Kushner began a writing career. His first work was *Namath, My Son Joe*, a collaboration with famed Jet quarterback Joe Namath's mother, Rose. Kushner then collaborated with Oakland Raiders hitman, Jack Tatum, and earned best-selling status with *They Call Me Assassin* (1980), and later on the sequel *They Still Call Me Assassin* (1989). Bill and Jack have their third book together entitled *FINAL CONFESSIONS of NFL Assassin Jack Tatum* (1996).

Bill Kushner also spent ten years with Hall Bartlett Films, and worked on and acted in Michael Landon's last made-for-television film, "Love is Forever." Bill recently completed a controversial biography, *The Way Things Oughta' Be TOLD* (1996), with former San Diego Charger, Burt Grossman; his first novel, *The Third Angel*; as well as this sports/inspirational biography entitled *A Reason to Believe: The Blaise Winter Story* (1998).

Amazing Golf Show and Clinic

If you're a convention/meeting planner, or golf tournament director, you're always asking yourself, *"Where do I find entertainment all my people will enjoy?"* The answer is Jim Chenoweth's one-man indoor (or outdoor) golfing show and clinic. Only a "pro's pro" like Jim could carry off his entertaining show that's guaranteed to "perk up" your group after hours of seminars and business speeches.

Jim is at ease at a seminar, a tournament clinic, or as an after-dinner or banquet attraction, and quickly wins over his audiences. He has appeared before groups from 25 to 2,000, but regardless of the size, the result is the same. They love him. Your group will, too.

"The clinic fit nicely into our overall program, and it was the unanimous feeling of all that we continue this activity in our annual program. Many thanks again for the very professional clinic you conducted."
– Lawrence J. Lombard, VP
Pepsi-Cola Company

"...the professional tips and interesting information that you provide golfers with during your clinic combine to make your program one of the most helpful and informative that any group could possibly enjoy, both from an entertaining and an educational standpoint..."
– Douglas A. Farley, CHSE, Director of Sales and Marketing
Aladdin Hotel Casino

Jim has had 45 years teaching experience. During his clinic he will show the perfect swing, proper placement of hands on the club, tips to a straighter, longer tee shot, the toe-up toe-up method, his simplified triangle swing concept, as well as, the scoring shots: putting, chipping, sand shots, etc. Following Jim's clinic, a question and answer session is held.

It's a hole-in-one, entertaining, 90-minute golf clinic.

For more information on the Golf Show and Clinic contact:
Jim Chenoweth Enterprises
P.O. Box 6661
Reno, Nevada 89513-9914
(702) 359-8143
Toll Free 1-888-465-3711

Instructional Video and Audio Tapes

Jim Chenoweth was named one of the "Top Teaching Professionals" in the U.S. on the *Mike Douglas Superstar Show* and *The Tonight Show*. He is a PGA golf pro who has been long regarded as one of America's top instructors.

His best-selling video tape "Video School of Golf" and his easy-to-understand audio tape "Mind Over Golf" have improved the games of thousands of golfers. Both tapes will take strokes off your score with Jim's proven, simplified golf swing technique and solid, down-to-earth advice that reveal the shot-saving secrets of the touring pros.

"Jim is the best instructor in the world."
— Rod Curl
PGA Tour Professional

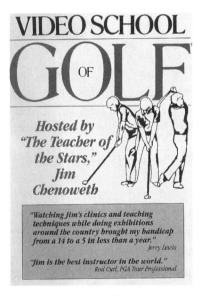

Take strokes off your score with Jim's proven, simplified golf swing technique.

Set of video and audio tapes, both for only $16.95 plus $2.00 shipping and handling.

To order Jim's tape set, please see the order form on page 256.

Another Great Golf Book
by Quality Sports Publications

**Terrific for young golfers, but beginning
golfers of all ages will love this book, too.**

"Tiger" is a lovable character who teaches golfers of all ages the game of golf. Intended to entice junior golfers to start out on the right foot, *Tiger's Tips* makes a perfect gift for everyone interested in taking up the game. After an overview, "Tiger" simplifies common golf terms. He then explains scorecards and holes, how golf clubs work, the golf swing, rules of the game, safety tips and etiquette. It instills confidence in young golfers before they hit the tee.

Tiger's Tips is full of helpful hints and answers to common questions and is filled with many photographs and hand drawn illustrations.

Tiger's Tips is only $10.95
plus $2.00 shipping and handling.

To order *Tiger's Tips*, please see the order form on page 256.

To receive a complimentary brochure on other
Quality Sports books, please call 1-800-464-1116.

ORDER FORM

Qty.	Title	Price	Total
	From Tee To Green To Hollywood	$16.95	
	Jim Chenoweth's Tape Set (audio & video)	$16.95	
	Tiger's Tips	$10.95	

Shipping and Handling Charges 1st product is $2.00 and each additional product only $1.00	Sub Total	
	Sales Tax (6.75% IL only)	
	← Shipping Cost	
	Total Cost	**$**

Please send my book(s) and/or tapes to the following address:

Name: _____ Phone #: (___) _____

Address: _____

City: _____ State: _____ Zip: _____

☐ Check or money order enclosed. Make checks payable to: *Quality Sports*

☐ Please charge my credit card

MasterCard ☐   Visa ☐   American Express ☐

Name as it appears on the card: _____

Credit card number: _____ Exp. date: _____

Signature: _____

TO ORDER BY CREDIT CARD, CALL TOLL FREE 1-800-464-1116

OR MAIL OR FAX FORM WITH PAYMENT TO:

Quality Sports Publications

24 Buysse Drive • Coal Valley, IL 61240

(800) 464-1116 • (309) 234-5016 • (309) 234-5019 FAX

BOOKS/TAPES WILL ARRIVE WITHIN 7 DAYS FROM YOUR ORDER.